The Power of the Dog

By

Ellen Dryden

FIRST
WRITES

First Writes Books Norfolk 2003

First Writes Books. Norfolk 2003

First Writes Books are published by
First Writes Theatre Company Ltd.
Lime Kiln Cottage, High Starlings
Banham. Norwich NR16 2BS

Printed by The Morris Printing Co.
57-61 Pitt Street, Norwich NR3 IDE

ISBN 1 901071 00 6

The Power of the Dog was first presented at the **Orange Tree Theatre**, Richmond, on May 9th 1996, with the following cast:

Vivien	Joan Moon
Grace	Barbara Lott
Vera	Georgine Anderson
Allan	Simon Chandler
Lisa	Louisa Milwood-Haigh
Richard	James Kerr

Designed by Sam Dowson

Lighting by Joe White

Directed by Sam Walters

For
Lincoln and Jonathan

THE POWER OF THE DOG

By Ellen Dryden

ACT ONE

We are in the sitting room of a small cottage, sparely furnished in a rather old-fashioned style, and obsessively neat and clean. The evening sun slants in through a window, bathing the set with a warm glow. It is all very peaceful and attractive, with gleaming brass, china and bowls of flowers. No petals have been allowed to fall on the polished surfaces and the cushions are carefully plumped up. The room is quite large and at some time has obviously been constructed from two separate cottages. One area of the room is a level higher than the other and there are two steps running the whole width of the room, dividing it in two. There are no books to be seen anywhere. An ornate old-fashioned upright piano stands, unopened, upstage.

*In the upper half of the cottage room, Grace, a lively, energetic woman in her seventies, is sitting in a wheel chair. She has an electric plug clamped between her knees and is attacking it clumsily, but with great determination, with an over-large screwdriver. Down the two shallow steps in the other half of the room is a large TV set. From it comes the sound of the hymn, **Dear Lord and Father of Mankind** being beautifully and fervently sung. After a moment Vivien comes in. She is in her forties, self assured, intelligent and detached. She is unobtrusively well-dressed and is carrying a small overnight bag. She stands watching quizzically for a moment*

1

VIVIEN: Are you reverting? Or entering your dotage…

GRACE: *(Looking up)* Oh it's you. Not before time. Switch that bloody thing off would you? Vera's gone to Church and she put it on for me while she was out.

> *Vivien crosses and switches off the set. Grace continues struggling with the plug.*

She only did it to annoy me. It's because I can't get down the steps. Every time she goes out she switches that damned set on and leaves me here, helpless, with some appalling tosh blaring out.

VIVIEN: Perhaps she thought **Songs of Praise** was appropriate.

GRACE: Hah! If it wasn't for the fact that she can't push this chair up the hill she'd have me in Church morning, noon and night thanking God for my miraculous recovery. Fortunately I only get to leave the house, at weekends, when Allan's around. He parks me in the saloon bar at **The Crooked Billet -** with the other geriatrics - ow!

> *Her hand slips with the screwdriver and she jabs it into her leg. She winces with pain. It is apparent that she has little or no movement in her right side. She speaks with care as if to conceal any weakness. Vivien crosses and looks at her closely.*

VIVIEN: What are you doing? Here. Give it to me!

GRACE: *(Aggressively rubbing her leg)* No. It's my therapy. I've got to try and get the movement back in this side.

VIVIEN: *(Incredulous)* And the doctor told you to sit there and fiddle about with electric plugs?!

GRACE: No. That was my idea.

VIVIEN: I might have known. It's ludicrous! You couldn't change a plug *before* you had a stroke. And what's the good of getting some movement back if you give yourself gangrene, gouging great holes in your leg! And that screwdriver's far too big.

> *Grace lays the screwdriver down in her lap. She sits still for a moment, gathering her strength. It is obvious that she*

is making strenuous efforts to behave as normally as possible. But this takes all her energy and when she relaxes for a moment everything about her sags.

GRACE: They are stupid fiddly things aren't they? You'd think they'd have invented something better by now.

VIVIEN: *(Watching her closely)* Why struggle with it then? Why not get something else? I could probably get you - oh I don't know - some of those children's developmental toys -

GRACE: *(Spikily)* Thank you very much. Every inch the school teacher! If you can't do something, lower your standards! I am trying to do this plug *because* I couldn't do them before! I've got to get out of this chair somehow.

VIVIEN: Mother you're mad.

GRACE: No I'm not. But I will be if I'm stuck here with Vera much longer. *(Pausing. And then, carefully)* Is that all the luggage you've got?

VIVIEN: Yes.

GRACE: Not planning on staying long then?

VIVIEN: I can't. I have to be back tomorrow.

GRACE: I see. *(Briskly)* Allan's staying at the moment. Don't lend him any money.

VIVIEN: There's no danger of that. Where is he?

GRACE: Gone to Church with Vera.

VIVIEN: Good God. What's he after?

GRACE: Redemption presumably.

VIVIEN: Huh! Surely even God has his limits?

GRACE: Theologically speaking no. But Allan can bleat as hard as he likes, he'll still end up with the goats.

> *She picks up her screwdriver and attacks the plug again. Vivien laughs. After a moment Grace joins in. Vivien looks at her a little awkwardly, then kisses the top of her head.*

VIVIEN: It's good to see you again. And looking so... cheerful.

GRACE: Make the most of it. Vera's angling to have me put away.

VIVIEN: Oh don't be ridiculous. She can't do that!

GRACE: Oh can't she! She's a very determined woman your Auntie Vera. And she has the sublime certainty of the im-impenetrably stupid to protect her. Every day she leaves me here with something that she knows will reduce me to gibbering rage - she puts that machine on - she puts my books away somewhere and she leaves my stuff just out of reach. Then she goes and tells everyone in the village that all I do is sit here and moan and snap at her. And she smiles her saintly Christian smile and says, yes it is a burden, but I am her only sister and she couldn't live with her conscience if she didn't do all she could for me, but she is worried about - lowering her voice dramatically - my mental state... The stroke seems to have affected my mind!

VIVIEN: *(Thoughtfully)* Yes... I can just see it.

GRACE: She's terrified I'll end up like darling Mummy.

VIVIEN: Oh for God's sake!

GRACE: *(Awkwardly)* You've got to help me, Vivien... There's nothing wrong with my mind yet, but there will be if I can't get away...

VIVIEN: Yes. We shall have to think of something.

> *There is an uneasy pause. Grace looks at her ironically.*

Do you want a cup of tea?

GRACE: Not particularly. But do make one for yourself if you want to. And, if it would make you feel better to feed one to the invalid, I'll drink it. *(Drily)* Mine's the cup with the bunny rabbits and the spout.

VIVIEN: I won't bother then. *(Looking at her watch.)* Anyway, Vera should be back soon.

GRACE: Not if she's doing good works on the way home. She's taken to performing little acts of loving kindness all round the village. With any luck someone will dash her brains out.

> *Vivien raises an eyebrow.*

GRACE: Oh don't mind me. It's my innate nastiness coming out... *(Echoing Vera)*'When people are faced with a burden to bear we see their true natures!' And of course, all these pills I'm taking make me depressed - 'it's only natural.' Vera's *very* understanding. She's practising being an amateur saint at the moment - and like all saints she's making everybody else's life intolerable.

VIVIEN: I see.

GRACE: No you don't. Don't you start humouring me... What time have you got to go tomorrow?

VIVIEN: Afternoon... *(Pause)* I could stay till evening I suppose -

GRACE: When does term start?

VIVIEN: A week on Thursday.

GRACE: Oh... Quite a while. I see.

VIVIEN: No you don't. Stop pretending to be Vera. You know perfectly well that teaching isn't just short days and long holidays. I've got a hell of a lot to do. I'm trying to do two jobs at once at the moment... The new Head doesn't just turn up on the first day of term and take it from there!

GRACE: I didn't know you were starting this new job now.

VIVIEN: Yes you did. I wrote and told you. Or don't you read my letters?

GRACE: I have been rather ill - unless it's escaped your notice. It's a perfectly ridiculous idea starting in the Summer Term. Why can't you wait till the Autumn and do things properly ?

VIVIEN: *(Tartly)* If I thought you were interested I'd tell you.

GRACE: Oh don't start sulking... You were always a dreadfully sulky little girl.

VIVIEN: How would you know? Any more from you and I'll put **Songs of Praise** back on.

GRACE: You'll have to, anyway. Vera will be back soon.

> *There is a pause.*

GRACE: *(Querulously)* I didn't know you were starting this new job now. I don't remember any letter... Mind you Vera doesn't give me all my post. She was offended when I wouldn't let her read them to me. I think she throws them away.

VIVIEN: I don't think she'd go that far.

GRACE: Oh yes she would! Aren't you a little too ready to take people at their own valuation to be a really good Headmistress? Oh I beg your pardon. Am I allowed to say that? What are you now - a Head Teacher? - or just a disembodied Head?

VIVIEN: I begin to sympathize with Vera.

GRACE: You must help me to get these things right. Perhaps you're Head Counsellor. I've just got used to telling people 'Oh no. My daughter's not an English Teacher. She's a Deputy Head, Pastoral Care, and she does a little teaching on the side. I understand some of her pupils can even read... Simple books of course.' I don't see why school teachers should have to behave like unskilled social workers. You just went to School to learn a few useful facts and mildly decent behaviour in my day - not to have your personality rummaged about in by well-meaning amateurs who can't manage to get their own lives in order. The net result of your interfering is that you turn out a bunch of illiterate misfits, instead of decently unhappy people who can read enough to sort out their own misery. My old Latin Teacher used to say 'Education is casting imitation pearls before real swine.' Seems to me nowadays all you're bent on doing is showing the Gadarene swine the quickest path to the cliff top!

> *She is speaking with a kind of quiet, desperate intensity, her words masking what she is really feeling. It becomes increasingly difficult for her to speak at all.*

VIVIEN: *(Soothingly)* Oh, come on, Mother. Don't - don't upset yourself. What are you getting so worked up for? You're not bothered about - Mother. You're - Oh no. *(Coldly)* Don't cry.

GRACE: Why not? Haven't I got enough to cry about? Oh don't worry. It won't bring on another stroke and if it does it will probably be fatal. With any luck! I can't do anything for myself. I'm stuck here with Vera... and you - you come here

6

and - you've plenty of time for your little no-hope waifs and strays but when it comes to your own mother you can only spare half an hour... Oh God, I don't mean that. I didn't want to say that -

VIVIEN: *(Remotely)* If it's what you feel it's as well you did.

GRACE: Don't talk to me in your phone-in Counsellor voice. I'm not one of your brain-damaged -

She stops and laughs painfully.

Yes. I am. That's exactly what I am. Brain-damaged. Literally.

She stops, bleakly unamused, as well as exhausted, by what she has said.

VIVIEN: *(Carefully)* Don't. There's no need to dramatise - I don't need shocking. I did see you at your worst, you know. You're making a remarkably good recovery.

GRACE: Thank you, dear. Good of you to let me know.

VIVIEN: You can speak. You've got a good deal of movement back -

GRACE: You're too kind. What a good job you weren't bright enough to go in for medicine. I'm overwhelmed by all this daughterly sympathy.

VIVIEN: I get it from you. I seem to recollect your telling me when I broke both legs that it needn't prevent me using my hands and my brains.
Grace laughs.

GRACE: Oh Vivien, I'm glad you've come. You're an appalling daughter but anything's better than Vera.

VIVIEN: And you're a self-centred old bat!

GRACE: Yes. You get that from me as well *(Lightly)* You can't imagine the horrors of being looked after by Vera. Will you - at least - help me to bath while you're here? Please. It's a ritual - ritual - humiliation when Vera does it... Decades of - venom in the way she pulls off my clothes and dumps me in the water - usually too hot - The saintly mask slips when there's only me to see it. She washes me... Then she leaves me... till the water's cold and I have to shout for her. She doesn't actually go into the village. But she goes as far down the garden as she can... I dislike it very much indeed.

>*Pause.*

VIVIEN: *(Neutrally)* Yes. I'm sure. I can remember what Vera's like. Don't flatter yourself that her little unkindnesses are specially thought out for you. She has a wide range she applies pretty universally. Age or state of health irrelevant.

GRACE: No. She has a strict hierarchy of diseases. Cancer is a cross inflicted on the noble in spirit so that they can be wonderfully brave. But strokes and senile dementia are a punishment for a selfish life, spent with your nose stuck in a book. Haven't you noticed how often it's 'really intelligent people' who get Alzheimer's disease? Vera has... She's got a list. She makes a point of telling me about all the famous -

VIVIEN: Don't worry. It's not - *(Choosing her words carefully)* unarguably - hereditary.

GRACE: Don't be patronising. Vera is the cross I have to bear. My punishment for being an inadequate mother. *(Ruefully)* Inadequate mothers make inadequate daughters.

VIVIEN: Never mind. I'll give you the odd break from Vera. To preserve your sanity - but more than that I cannot do at the moment.

GRACE: Good. I'll look forward to it. It'll be a pleasant change. This place is full of brainless young hausfraus who've been dumped here by their husbands. *They* spend all week in town making money and God knows what else. Vera's got the hausfraus to put me on their list after the Natural Childbirth Rummage Sales and the Green Party Camomile Tea Mornings. They whizz round in their Range Rovers stopping the locals putting up satellite dishes. They all have hoards of appalling children called Barnaby, or Emily. They just love living in the country. They think all I want to do is teach their wretched offspring how to do recycled jigsaw puzzles, or listen to them playing the oboe. Ghastly little hypocrites sit there saying, 'Mummy says I mustn't have that if it's not organic.' Then the minute Mummy's back is turned they rush in here, wolf down all those disgusting Fondant Fancies Vera is so partial to, and watch **Neighbours** - Polluting body and soul at one fell swoop.

VIVIEN: I'm surprised Vera lets them.

GRACE: They're such a nice class of person. How Vera's always seen herself. I ought to be grateful that all these young things want to bother with a miserable old woman like me. Makes them feel really good, you see, doing their neighbourly duty.

VIVIEN: *(Drily)* Well. I promise you. It won't make me feel good.

GRACE: Then I shall take the opportunity to be as difficult as possible. Just drive me somewhere I can sit and scream and smash things.

VIVIEN: You'd better come to school with me.

GRACE: The day before yesterday one of Vera's ministering angels came round and said she'd dumped the children for the day and would I like to go to the new Garden Centre with her. I told her I loathed Garden Centres with an intensity that was only equalled by my loathing of the people who go to them. So she laughed and said 'Oh Grace, you are wonderful. I hope I'm like you when I'm your age.' I told her not to be impertinent and would she please call me Mrs Harper.

VIVIEN: And?

GRACE: She laughed merrily and she and Vera manhandled me into the Range Rover. She pushed me round the wretched place for two hours in the blazing sun. I put the brake on when she wasn't looking. She bought me some dreadful, lurid petunias in a vulgar imitation urn. They were half-price because they were half-dead. She thought they would brighten my outlook. Spiritual or actual I have no idea.

There is the sound of a door banging offstage.

She's back. Put that thing back on -

She picks up her plug and screwdriver again and sits hunched in her wheelchair. She seems to have shrunk into herself. Vivien, slightly surprised, crosses and switches on the television. Allan and Vera come in, as the programme continues.

9

Vera is Grace's younger sister. She is in her late sixties. She is very carefully and well dressed and is carrying a prayer book - the picture of respectability. Allan is her son. In his mid thirties, he is secretive, watchful and defensive. He is good-looking and casually dressed as if to emphasise the differences between his mother and himself. His attitude to Vera and Grace is one of a delicate, and not altogether pleasant, mockery which expresses itself in charming deference.

TV VOICE: And now on this glorious evening as the sun goes down into the sea in a blaze of golden light and the shadows lengthen on the hillside - the beauty of this scene reminding us of God's eternal gifts to us, his poor sinful flock, let us sing together, in God's open air, that beautiful old hymn **We thank thee, Lord, for this Fair Earth.**

VERA: Oh hello, Vivien. You managed to get here then. We were expecting you this afternoon.

Vivien and Vera exchange a perfunctory 'kiss'

VIVIEN: Hello, Vera, you're looking well.

VERA: What was the traffic like?

VIVIEN: Not too bad. Hello Allan.

VERA: Oh this is one of my favourites!

She turns up the television a little and joins in the singing. The others wait around rather awkwardly.

VERA: Have you had anything to eat?

VIVIEN: I did stop for a sandwich on the way up...

ALLAN: Tch! Tch! Even so you'll have to finish up the scones and bridge rolls we got ready for you at tea time.

VERA: For Goodness' sake, Allan, we do usually manage to have a decent tea on a Sunday - whether Vivien's here or not! Oh isn't that a picture? Isn't it beautiful? Where is it? *(Pause.)* Where is it, Grace?

GRACE: What?

VERA: *(Patiently)* The Television. Where is that? Where's the service coming from.

GRACE: I don't know.

Vera, behind Grace's back, casts expressive glances at Vivien and Allan.

VERA: *(With a little laugh)* 'I don't know'! You've been sitting here watching it for the last half hour and you don't know where it is!

VIVIEN: Looks like Devon -

VERA: Devon is a very big county! I don't know, Grace, you get worse.

She switches off the TV with a snap.

VERA: I thought you enjoyed the hymns.

Grace says nothing.

VIVIEN: I'm afraid I came in and switched it off, Vera. Mother and I have been chatting.

ALLAN: And then, it switched itself back again on as we came through the door...

Vivien looks coldly at him. He smiles.

VERA: Well, I'm glad you could get a word out of her anyway. How do you think she's looking?

VIVIEN: Pretty well.

GRACE: What's the time?

VIVIEN: Just coming up to half-past seven.

GRACE: I should have had my tablets twenty minutes ago.

VERA: All right, all right! You don't have to take them to the minute! I wasn't here twenty minutes ago was I?... If you're so fussy you could have asked Vivien.

GRACE: My daughter hasn't come here to dole out my medicines.

VERA: We all know that, don't we?

She goes out.

ALLAN: I don't think Mother enjoyed the service very much tonight. It was a United Service and the Church was full of ranting

11

Methodists... I'm speaking metaphorically, of course, there must have been... oh... at least thirty of us! The sermon was one of those uncomfortable affairs. The preacher attacked everybody for wearing their best clothes in Church and went on - approvingly - about Jesus' unfortunate habit of mixing with publicans and sinners. He was very pro sinners - though I should think *his* greatest sin was riding his bike without lights... One of those etiolated youths with glasses, and, I suspect, an engineering degree. I do mistrust the young when they get religion. Mother detected an ever so slightly common tinge to his accent. She didn't say anything, but looks were exchanged with Mrs Tarrant. Fortunately it doesn't happen too often. There'll be no more unseemly enthusiasm next week... *(Sweetly)* Will you still be here then, Vivien?

VIVIEN: No.

> *Vera has returned with a bottle of pills and a glass of water. She hands the pill bottle to Grace who takes it and rather surreptitiously attempts to open it herself. Vera stands holding the glass of water, but looking at Vivien.*

VERA: How long are you staying, Vivien?

VIVIEN: *(With a glance at Grace)* Tomorrow. Or - or - Tuesday.

VERA: Well, I was going to put you in your old room - but I've got all my sewing things in there. It doesn't seem worth clearing them all out for such a short time. You wouldn't mind having the bed-settee in here, would you?

ALLAN: I'm in the spare bedroom you see - and I'd hate to sleep on the bed-settee.

VIVIEN: *(Evenly)* I don't mind where I sleep. Don't put yourself out, Vera.

VERA: When do you go back to school, Vivien? The children round here have got another two weeks.

VIVIEN: *(Pleasantly)* Yes so have we. But I'm starting a new job. I've been appointed Head of a school in South London.

VERA: I thought you liked it where you are.

VIVIEN: Yes Well, I do - did. But I wasn't the Head. The new school is in a bit of a mess. It's a challenge.

ALLAN: Which came first? The career move - or your missionary instincts? Going into darkest South London and bringing them the true word?

VIVIEN: I wouldn't pursue that line of thought, if I were you, Allan.

VERA: If the school's in such a mess, why haven't they appointed a man?

VIVIEN: Because it was a man who made such a mess of it in the first place.

VERA: It's a mixed school?

VIVIEN: Yes. Very.

VERA: I don't mean to be rude, but it seems extraordinary to me. You're far too young. That's the trouble nowadays. Headmistresses used to be people you could look up to - dignified... older...

VIVIEN: I think that was a trick of the light. Thirty five's the end of the line as far as the young are concerned - in spite of all the wishful thinking about the fascinating over-fifties!

ALLAN: It's all of a piece with callow youths telling you that putting a fiver in the collection plate doesn't automatically book your passage to Heaven isn't it, Ma?

GRACE: *(Petulantly)* Vera. I cannot open this wretched bottle. You know I can't.

> *She flings the pill bottle across the room. There is a shocked pause. Vera looks impassive. Vivien retrieves the bottle, and holds it at arm's length.*

VIVIEN: Here we are. Oh God! I'm not so young *I* can read this without my glasses. What is it? Two? I do loathe these childproof tops.

GRACE: *(Angrily)* Stop humouring me! If you can't read the - you can't mend a plug - you can't get the top off a pill bottle! Neither can I! I can't get out of this damned chair either! Stop pretending. Why don't you have your own stroke - you've got all the symptoms - if it's so bloody normal?

VERA: *(Icily)* Don't swear, Grace. It's very unpleasant in a woman of your age. I am not having scenes. Allan, take your Aunt Grace for a walk. She needs the fresh air and the chance to calm down and behave properly. No, Grace, don't say anything. Just be careful. You'll undo months of patient, hard work if you go on like this. It's a nice evening. A walk will do you good. And I want to talk to Vivien. Allan. Please.

ALLAN: Of course. Come on, Auntie Grace. You'd better have these first.

He takes the pill bottle from Vivien and shakes out two tablets. Vera hands him the glass of water. They stand either side of the wheelchair while Grace obediently swallows the tablets. Vivien turns away. Vera takes the pill bottle and the glass out into the kitchen. Allan pushes Grace out.

ALLAN: *(As they go):* Your coat's in the hall, isn't it? You won't need your gloves. It's quite mild.

Vera returns.

VIVIEN: I'm sorry. I'm afraid I provoked that...

VERA: *(Sitting down wearily)* Oh no. I'm afraid they're getting to be a daily occurrence - these tantrums. Everything you do for her - well, nothing's ever right. I'm afraid I can't get a pleasant word out of her. In fact I can hardly get a word out of her at all. Did she say much to you?

VIVIEN: Yes. She was quite chatty... She seemed a lot better. Almost her old self.

VERA: Ah well, you don't see the half of it. She might seem like that - in short bursts - but most of the time - well, just let me say, it's very, very difficult.

VIVIEN: Yes I can imagine...

VERA: I'm glad you got the chance to see her, on her own. Don't you think she's altered? I can't pretend I'm not worried about her.

Vivien does not reply for a moment. She seems uncertain what to say. Vera continues.

Perhaps I ought to try to be a bit tougher. But, it's very difficult - being treated like, well, *dirt* day in, day out. Grace

14

is my only sister and this is her home, but she can be very rude - very hurtful when she likes. I'm doing my best, Vivien - nobody could do more. I know you can't get down very often. You've got a busy life and this new job must be a big strain. I don't expect you to -

VIVIEN: Vera, I can't - physically - do any more at the moment. I can't really afford the time to be here now. I've taken on an enormous new job. In fact I'm doing two jobs at once. Falling between two schools...

Vera does not respond. Vivien knows she is chattering on but cannot seem to stop.

I mustn't fail. I'm moving house - without any great success - or trying to. The gap between what I can afford and what I would like to live in... Grace isn't the only -

VERA: No, no, you don't understand. I realise how difficult it all is for you. As long as I am capable of it I shall do my best for Grace. I always have and I can't see that changing at my time of life. Grace has always had that way with her. People do things for her. But she's very ungracious about it sometimes. Grace by name but not by nature.

It is obvious Vivien has heard this before.

I shall never forget the time she came back on furlough when I was looking after you. I'd bought you that lovely blue spotted dress with the smocking and she just looked at you and said 'Good heavens Vera, what are you doing to my daughter? Trying to turn her into Shirley Temple?' I didn't say anything but I was very hurt. Grace has always gone her own way regardless. Mother used to say she saved up all her kindness for people she didn't know! Goodness knows what she was like with the poor heathen! I hope she treated them better than her own family. But I'm used to it now.

VIVIEN: I don't really remember that. I remember the frock - I think I do...

VERA: I remember it all very clearly. You wouldn't wear it again. I gave it to Mrs Parsons for Hazel.

VIVIEN: Well, we've established that Mother's always been difficult. She's had a stroke. She seems to be making a good recovery.

Is there a new problem? Do you need a break? I can't do anything myself at the moment but I could organize someone - professionally, I mean, to relieve you -

VERA: Absolutely not! While I've got my strength I am not having paid help to look after a member of my family. You can laugh at me if you like. I know it's old-fashioned but I do believe in doing my Christian duty.

VIVIEN: Yes. I know. I'm sorry, I didn't mean to upset you. You've always been - *(She hesitates)* - wonderful... but... What was it you wanted to talk to me about? If there's a problem let's sort it out.

VERA: *(With a little laugh)* Oh, every inch the headmistress! I'm quite afraid of you!

VIVIEN: *(Shortly):* There's no need.

VERA: Well. I am concerned there's no denying it. She's a difficult person. You say she's always been difficult... Well, yes, but she's changing... She's not the person she used to be... She's difficult in a different way now... She doesn't read or listen to the wireless any more... She won't listen to any of her music. She just sits there fiddling with electric plugs and silly things like that... She really snaps at me if I try to take them from her - apart from that she hardly ever speaks to me. And her memory! Well, you saw that!

VIVIEN: What?

VERA: Just now. She hadn't got the slightest idea what was going on, on the TV. She'd been sitting in front of it for over an hour!

VIVIEN: That could be a sign of acute discrimination!

VERA: I'm sure that's very clever but the fact remains -

VIVIEN: The fact remains that *I* turned the television off. I haven't the slightest idea what was on... hymns or something..

VERA: She told you to turn it off though didn't she? That's another thing - anything at all, the least bit religious and she flies into a rage. You should hear the language if I suggest taking her to Church... She won't go to any of the services - no matter how hard I try. We had a meeting the other week - a young missionary gave a talk about her work in Africa, with films

16

and slides and everything. She was a really up-to-date, modern-looking young woman. Not at all what you'd expect. I suggested Grace should come along and share her experiences. It would have been interesting and it would have done Grace good to get out for a bit. Not just sit here thinking about herself all the time. But she was quite short with me. In fact she was really nasty. I couldn't see what I was doing wrong, frankly. After all Grace was a missionary herself.

VIVIEN: Dad was a missionary. Grace was his wife.

VERA: Oh no! You were only a little girl. You didn't see the half of it. Andrew was a wonderful Christian man. They went everywhere together. He worked himself to death. And your mother worked with him. You don't lead a life like that unless you believe in it.

VIVIEN: I couldn't certainly. But perhaps she could.

VERA: I think that's a dreadful thing to say. And I think it's terrible that after a life of service, Grace is Godless now.

VIVIEN: *(Ironically)* She did - how shall I put it? - lose her faith pretty smartly after Dad died.

VERA: No, she was grieving. That's only natural. *(Carefully)* What I'm talking about now is - well - a whole series of very worrying changes... in her whole personality. I'm surprised you couldn't see it.

VIVIEN: *(Brutally)* Are you trying to imply that she's got Alzheimer's disease?

VERA: *(After a brief pause)* I couldn't possibly say. But after what I suffered with poor Mother... I couldn't go through that again. I was a younger woman then and it nearly broke me... I can't do it again, I'm afraid...

VIVIEN: I don't think there is the slightest sign that there is anything like that wrong with mother. Her mind seems particularly sharp to me. And her memory. As you say - or as you imply - she has always been selfish *(She laughs slightly)* The selfish missionary! She is difficult, and a very bad patient. I can imagine you're having a tough time with her... And - for whatever reason - she... renounced religion when my father died. I don't think it's wise to question her religious beliefs - or unbeliefs. It's perfectly possible to lead a quite normal life and never set foot in the Church. *(Lightly)* I'm an atheist myself. I don't think that makes me certifiable.

VERA: Your unbelief doesn't mean God doesn't exist. And the Devil can still speak through you. I don't think it's at all clever to talk like that. But then talking doesn't solve very much does it? If you want to blind yourself to what is happening to your mother - well all I can say is, you're not here day by day and you can't see what I see.

VIVIEN: No. I can't see into your heart and mind, either, Vera. Though your God presumably can. And our differing perceptions of the problem that is my mother don't actually solve anything - practical - do they?

VERA: There isn't a practical problem - for you. I shall continue to look after Grace. On my own if necessary.

VIVIEN: Vera. There is no need -

VERA: I haven't got anything more to say.

> *She goes out, near to tears.*

VIVIEN: *(Resignedly)* Oh God! Go out, Vivien, come back in and start again! And see if you can get nowhere even faster.

> *Vivien crosses to the bed-settee, which is just that, not a sofa-bed, being defiantly old-fashioned, and flings her bag onto it. She stands looking down at it, a rueful expression on her face. Allan enters noiselessly, sees Vivien and grins maliciously.*

ALLAN: Allow me.

> *He crosses, removes Vivien's bag and deftly pulls out the strap that opens out the bed. He wrinkles his nose fastidiously.*

Bad luck!

VIVIEN: So I'm in the punishment block?

ALLAN: Well, if you will pay these fleeting visits...

VIVIEN: And the spare room is full. I presume Vera is embroidering a handkerchief in there.

ALLAN: A tray-cloth. For the Church Bazaar. At Christmas.

VIVIEN: *(With feeling)* Oh God, I hate this thing. It's all right for you. You didn't have to face being dragged down here every time there was anything remotely the matter with you. I've had chicken pox, measles, swollen glands, whooping cough and every known cold virus on there. Nothing to read, nothing to do, feeling bloody and Vera coming in at ten minute intervals to pour cod-liver oil down my throat and put scalding hot kaolin poultices round my neck and feed me bread and milk. Ugh! I used to try to keep the cod-liver oil in my mouth and spit it down the side when she wasn't looking. That's probably why it stinks. But I think it just preserved the leatherette. Can't you persuade her to get rid of it? I have an overwhelming, irrational terror of the thing.

ALLAN: Vivien, what an immoral suggestion! That is a good solid piece of furniture. It's not one of these nasty modern things. All foam and no substance. Mother paid a lot of money for that when she could ill afford it and it will see her out!

VIVIEN: It'll see me out sooner. Where's Grace?

ALLAN: In her room.

VIVIEN: How do you think she is?

ALLAN: Better than she pretends to be.

VIVIEN: That was my impression. It's not what Vera thinks.

ALLAN: My Mother is only truly fulfilled when tending to the sick and needy.

VIVIEN: I know. It chills the blood. 'It doesn't matter how intelligent you think you are, we're all equal when we're poorly.'

ALLAN: Oh yes. 'The cleverest people are just babies when they've got tummy-ache.' *(Pause)* I wanted a word with you - not unrelated - about all that.

VIVIEN: Now?

ALLAN: Oh no. And preferably not here. Perhaps we could slip out to the **Billet** -

VIVIEN: Going to the pub on Sunday, Allan? Tchk! Tchk! OK. Why not? What's it all about?

ALLAN: Later.

VIVIEN: Well, I warn you, I've reached cut-off point with personal problems.

ALLAN: Oh so have I. You know I'm living here at the moment?

VIVIEN: *(Surprised)* No I didn't. Where's... Paula?

ALLAN: *(With a grin)* Annette, Vivien, Annette. Paula was my first ex-wife.

VIVIEN: Again? Allan, how do you manage to get yourself entangled with these brainless trollops?

ALLAN: I get bemused with lust. And I'm afraid they're seldom trollops. I seem to be turned on by petit bourgeois morality. They usually have a devastating streak of respectability which requires marriage. The woman tempted me and I did sign up for the endowment mortgage. *(Thoughtfully)* Vera likes Annette even less than Paula. And of course the wedding was a horrible hole-in-the-corner affair in a registry office. You must remember. We didn't invite you... Divorce is so painful. And every time you split up the marital home you're left with half the number you first thought of. So I had to come home to mother.

VIVIEN: And Vera wouldn't subsidise you if you just shacked up with them.

ALLAN: A little crude, but you cut through to the essentials so quickly. She has a warm maternal understanding of my problems. She hates to see me bamboozled by these avaricious females. They trap me by my chivalrous nature into matrimony. None of them will ever see thirty again...

VIVIEN: You'll have to break away from the Annettes and Paulas of this world, Allan. You'd get a better class of bimbo if you moved into the Sophie/Caroline market.

ALLAN: I don't think mother would enjoy that very much. She likes to feel that I've married beneath me. And what sort of talk is that for the Headmistress of a down-market Comprehensive?

VIVIEN: *(With a smile)* I'm on holiday.

ALLAN: Aren't you the lucky one! I of course am between jobs as well as wives.

VIVIEN: Well, there's a surprise.

ALLAN: I blame you, of course. You should have taken my emotional development in hand, as it were, when I was a palpitating adolescent and you were a beautiful young widow. It was very selfish of you... I made it very clear I was available for a sentimental education. All you did was shatter my fragile confidence and give me a life-long terror of intelligent women.

VIVIEN: Don't like it when we see through you? As I remember, you were a nauseating little boy, a corrupt adolescent and now you're a pathetic -

She looks at him speculatively and shrugs.

man!

ALLAN: The crowning insult. Careful. If Mummy heard you talking to me like that she'd have Grace on pin-down till Christmas. I'm afraid Vera's right though, Vivien. All this education has made you very hard. Grace is much more fun, but I don't think she likes me as much as you do.

Vivien smiles at him.

VIVIEN: You may be devious - but at least you're straightforward about it. Which is a relief. I don't know how long I can keep walking on eggshells with Vera.

ALLAN: Don't bother. It doesn't matter what you say. She doesn't like you. You shouldn't have put me in the shade. My genius is rebuked by you.

VIVIEN: No it isn't. You're just incredibly lazy.

ALLAN: Ah yes. Which creates the bigger balls-up do you suppose? Seizing life by the throat and making decisions in all directions. Or letting the tide take you?

His voice is very bitter. There is a pause.

VIVIEN: *(Wryly)* I suspect it's roundabouts and swings.

Pause.

ALLAN: So you'll take me out for a drink at **The Crooked Billet** later on then?

VIVIEN: I suppose a few gins might anæsthetize me for this. *(Gesturing towards the sofa)...* All right.

ALLAN: Good.

Allan looks at her speculatively for a moment, then goes. Vivien stands lost in thought beside the bed. The lights fade slightly. Grace silently wheels herself in, upstage, and sits watching. The two women do not acknowledge, indeed are not aware of, each other's presence.

VIVIEN: *(Remotely)* Dearest Vivien, The quickest of notes for now. There's no time for a proper letter. I'll write you a lovely long one later on when I'm not so busy. Daddy and I are getting settled in nicely into our mud hut! No! It's not squelchy wet mud like you're used to. It's packed hard. And then we give it a skimming of cow-dung - yes cow dung! - then whitewash it. You'd be amazed how elegant we are. Daddy's working very hard - getting up at four o' clock helping to build the new road and clear the ground for planting. Tea, strawberries and potatoes. Doesn't that sound like home? But there's miles and miles of them here. I hope you are being a good girl and working hard at school. I have asked Auntie Vera to buy a birthday present for you from Daddy and me, so you tell her what you would like. Have a lovely time - Lots of Love, Mummy. PS Daddy sends you a thousand kisses.

The lights fade on the cottage, leaving Grace sitting motionless, in the darkened room.
The scene changes to Vivien's study, at school, which, by means of a truck, or revolve, occupies the lower level of the stage. It is a small, functional room, with a desk, two chairs and well-stocked bookshelves. There are posters and prints on the wall and healthy flowering plants stand on all available surfaces. It is basically a bare, institutional space, but it has been made into an attractive, welcoming, little study - one that it would be a pleasure to work in.

Vivien crosses, enters her study and stands with her back to the audience looking out of the window. She looks at her watch. She sees someone out of the window and goes to sit down on one of the two chairs. She picks up a book and is looking through it when Lisa comes in.

Lisa is seventeen. She is a slight, unremarkable-looking girl with a cold remote manner, which only imperfectly conceals a turbulent, intense interior. She has immense charm when she relaxes and laughs or even smiles - which is rare. At the moment she is very defensive. There is a long pause while Vivien looks at her.

LISA: Sorry I'm late.

Her voice is a suburban London whine.

VIVIEN: What is it this time?

LISA: I've been waiting at that bus stop thirty five minutes.

VIVIEN: It's only a ten minute walk.

LISA: You are joking!

VIVIEN: I have been sitting here for twenty minutes. I was about to go.

LISA: *(Aggressively)* Sorree!

Pause.

VIVIEN: If you can't be bothered to get here on time I can't be bothered to give up my time.

Lisa looks mutinously at her but says nothing.

LISA: Mum was being a bit stroppy as well. I had to calm her down.

VIVIEN: Is that true? Or do you think that's a good line to spin me?

LISA: It's a safe bet actually. My Mum's always stroppy.

VIVIEN: There's still no chance of her coming to see me?

LISA: Nah! She doesn't like schools. Give her panic attacks. *(Pause)* And I don't want you to come to my house.

VIVIEN: No.

Lisa turns her back. Then changes the subject with great energy.

LISA: Listen. I reckon you owe me ten quid. I went to see that **Midsummer Night's Dream.** It was crap! Helena was about thirty five, kept chucking herself all over the place - tossing her hair back and flinging her arms about. You know - just like young people always do when we're in love. Nearly ruptured herself. She was about six inches shorter than Hermia as well, so she'd got these gross high heels and Hermia had to bend at the knees all through the quarrel scene. And the Mechanicals wandered about in the audience and talked to us. I hate that! And Peter Quince sat in the Stalls and shouted his lines from there. And the fairies all lived in cardboard boxes and had tattoos. Puck was a drug-pusher. And it went on for nearly four hours. I reckon ours was better. And I couldn't afford it!

VIVIEN: Sorry.

LISA: Hey and guess what! Theseus and Hippolyta played Oberon and Titania! Isn't that original? Everybody liked it except me. I wanted to get up and kill them all. Bunch of tossers.

VIVIEN: Fairly extreme critical reaction but I know what you mean.

LISA: Well it was everything you say was wrong -

VIVIEN: You mustn't just take my opinions -

LISA: I don't. You should know that. I agree with you sometimes. Sometimes I don't. But I really love that play... I don't think this had any... respect. And it wasn't - magic...

She stops, lost in thought for a moment.

I know. 'The best in this kind are but shadows and the worst no worse if imagination amend them... It must be your imagination then and not theirs.'

She is very still. Her face becomes a mask.

(Very quietly) I like - magic. *(Briskly)* I suppose I'm talking rubbish - everybody else says it's brilliant. And they're paid to be in the imagination business, aren't they? And I've got no right to criticize them.

VIVIEN: You know that's not the case. If you can support your opinions -

She stops abruptly and sits staring rather wearily at nothing. Lisa watches her.

LISA: What's the matter?

VIVIEN: Nothing. I just heard myself trotting out the old school teachers' clichés.

LISA: That's what you're paid for isn't it?

VIVIEN: I'm not paid at all for these sessions as it happens.

Lisa gives her a strangely frightened look but her manner becomes even more brusque.

LISA: Sorry. I didn't ask you to do it.

VIVIEN: No. No, you didn't.

She is standing with her back to Lisa.

(Remotely) You'd better read me your Jane Austen essay.

There is a long pause.

LISA: That could be difficult. I haven't written it yet.

Pause.

VIVIEN: What's the excuse this time?

LISA: *(Flaring up)* Which one would you like? I left my book on the bus? I was catching up on my German homework - that I have not done all term as Mrs Parker will be only too pleased to tell you? Or I was up all night with my mum who thought there were ten foot green spiders in the fridge? Or that I went down the pub with some of the few friends I've got left? Or I don't give a shit about 'Emma Woodhouse handsome rich and clever'? What's it got to do with me anyway? I sell light fittings at B&Q and live in a council flat don't I?

VIVIEN: Well done! It's an improvement on your usual excuses. Clever? You know very well that you are. Handsome? I suppose there are those that would say you are. Rich? Well you'll certainly never be that if you carry on wilfully destroying your only escape route. Somehow - somewhere along the line you have been blessed with a remarkable intelligence and I am not going to waste my time or yours pretending otherwise. If you want to squander it... It's up to you, if you want to stay in the wretched circumstances you are unfortunate enough to live in.

LISA: *(With a sudden grin)* Steady on. You're not supposed to say that - you should be all soothing and understanding, and ask me to write a few paragraphs - no - a few lines about EastEnders - 'cos that's my culture innit? *(With an abrupt change of mood)* You see - I have learned some of my lessons. I know I'm useless rubbish if I'm left to myself. Got to get the Jane Austen right, haven't I?

VIVIEN: Lisa. I do know you well enough to know when you are exercising your considerable abilities - to annoy - to distract me from the fact that once again you haven't written an essay I set you.

LISA: *(Flatly)* I meant to write it. And I didn't. I knew what I wanted to say. And I watched the telly.

> *Vivien is silent for a moment. She seems about to say something then changes her mind.*

VIVIEN: *(Briskly)* So we're wasting each other's time. You may as well go home.

LISA: *(Surprised)* I came in specially -

VIVIEN: Not specially enough. I'm not going to waste my spare time if you can't be bothered to do the work I set you. What's the point in bothering to turn up at all? You should catch the five o' clock bus if you leave now.

LISA: *(With a sort of desperation)* No. I don't want to go. This was your idea not mine... You've always made me work - You're just like all the others. Nobody ever wants to bother with me for long. *(Muttering aggressively)* Anyway. I've written a story...

VIVIEN: What?

LISA: I wrote a story. I was going to show it to you, but I don't suppose it's worth bothering with. I mean, it's not Jane Austen.

VIVIEN: No. I shouldn't think it is... Would you like to read it to me?

LISA: No. You can read it for yourself. I'd better be going then. I've got a lot to do.

VIVIEN: Lisa -

LISA: *(Savagely)* 'Lisa - listen to me. I can't do your work for you. There's only one person who can do that and that's you, yourself. Self discipline. blah blah blah..Letting yourself down blah blah blah.. Don't waste your talents blah blah blah...' Christ I wish I was thick!!

VIVIEN: No you don't.

> *Lisa stares at her mutinously. Vivien seems disinclined to respond to her outburst. She rises and moves away again, with her back to Lisa, who is becoming more and more ill at ease.*

VIVIEN: *(Distantly)* I'd like to read your story.

LISA: You'll have to ask Mrs Parker. It's in my German book.

VIVIEN: Oh Lisa, you little idiot. Why?

LISA: It was the only paper I'd got.

VIVIEN: Had you done your German homework?

LISA: No.

VIVIEN: You'd better. You're not going to get into University with one A-Level.

LISA: I'll only need two E's if they like me at Oxford University though won't I?

> *Her voice is full of contempt.*

VIVIEN: If. Don't run away with the idea it's a foregone conclusion. You do have to make a certain minimal effort yourself. There are things -

> *She is choosing her words carefully and Lisa stares at her slightly worried by the unexpected uncertainty from the normally decisive Vivien. There is a hammering at the door and, without waiting for a reply, Richard Shaw bursts in. A thin, impetuous, rather aggressive, young*

man, he is casually but not scruffily dressed. Always abrasive in manner, he is bitingly angry at the moment.

RICHARD: I want a word with you, Mrs Chadwick.

VIVIEN: Do you? *(Coldly)* Is it urgent?

RICHARD: Very.

VIVIEN: I see.

RICHARD: Wait outside, Lisa.

VIVIEN: As it happens, Lisa was just going.

LISA: *(Enjoying herself)* Oh. Was I?

VIVIEN: Yes. You've got an essay to write - or not, as the case may be.

RICHARD: Glad to see you still remember the way here, Lisa.

LISA: *(Sullenly)* I've had the 'flu. *(To Vivien)* Am I supposed to come next Monday?

VIVIEN: *(After a quick look at Richard)* Yes. If you want to. And if you've done your work.

LISA: Yes. Well. I'll try. But you don't know how hard it is.

> *She goes out quickly, leaving the door open. Richard crosses and closes it firmly behind her, making sure that she has really gone.*

VIVIEN: *(Coldly)* I would appreciate it if you didn't burst in here quite so tempestuously. Especially when I am teaching.

RICHARD: Oh. I beg your pardon. I was under the impression that School finished at quarter to four. And your A-Level class has shrunk, hasn't it?

VIVIEN: There is no need for this childishness, Richard. I believe I know why you want to see me.

RICHARD: Oh good! Well would you mind telling me what the hell you're playing at? I have just had one of the most humiliating interviews of my life. I was invited - no summoned - to the Head's office. In writing. For a drink and a chat after school. I go along expecting to discuss my promotion. Tchah! He really enjoyed himself watching me get the message. The bit he liked best was telling me this was all done with your connivance.

VIVIEN: The vindictive little sod. I am truly sorry, Richard. I asked him not to speak to you until I'd had a chance to discuss it with you.

RICHARD: I see. You're sorry that he put the boot in before you had the chance. *I'm* not one of your half-witted lame ducks. What are you doing discussing me in this tender fashion behind my back?

VIVIEN: That is a half-witted remark and you know it. It's my job to discuss your suitability as my successor. You're caught in the cross-fire and if you calmed down for a moment you would realise he is simply indulging in one of his petty little acts of malice to punish me for leaving. And if he can include you as well so much the better.

RICHARD: And what makes you think that makes a shred of bloody difference? He's a contemptible little shit. We all live with that. What I want to know is why you couldn't tell me to my face - before you went running to him - that I am totally unfitted to take over from you as Head of the Department. That you cannot give me any kind of recommendation. That I am too young. Too *volatile*!!

> *He spits out the word with real venom, but it is obvious that he is hurt by what he sees as Vivien's betrayal.*

Oh, it gave him a real thrill sitting there, spreading out his hands and telling me it was your assessment of me and wouldn't it be better if I withdrew my application - to avoid embarrassment! For Christ's sake, Viv, what are you up to? You bloody well appointed me - over his supine body!

VIVIEN: Has it not occurred to you that he was lying?

> *Richard is stopped in his tracks. He looks at Vivien, conflicting emotions expressing themselves on his face. Finally it is with an almost comic disgust that he speaks*

RICHARD: Lying? Oh come on. You must have said something - Even he wouldn't - Not so blatantly....

VIVIEN: Are you sure? *(Pause)* It's always worked before. The big lie. He's getting a bit careless though, it's worked so well. Other people are beginning to see through him. In fourteen years as Head nothing has ever been his fault. He has a wonderful gift for delegating blame. When the balloon goes up Macavity is never there.

RICHARD: *(Slowly)* Nevertheless. I can hear you saying all that about me.

VIVIEN: *(Wincing)* Don't say that, Richard. I would never discuss you - or anyone I respected - in those terms with -

She stops.

I used to think he was just hopeless. But he isn't. Like most incompetents in power, he's malignant as well.

RICHARD: *(Brusquely)* Even so. You must have said something. What was it? Or am I not allowed to know?

VIVIEN: All I said was - and this was some weeks ago, before you mentioned applying - that I didn't think it was in your best interests to take over from me.

RICHARD: Meaning?

VIVIEN: Wait a minute. When he asked me what I had to say about your application I said I didn't want to comment until I had spoken to you.

RICHARD: And?

VIVIEN: I would have done my best to persuade you not to apply for the job. This school is in savage decline. We spend all our teaching time coping with the latest bureaucratic idiocy and getting the blame for all society's ills, and nothing like enough time doing what we're here for. And in an already bad school that is unendurable. I don't think you should try to make a career here. You are - just - too young. You're a good teacher. You will obviously get your promotion very soon. But I think you should leave here as soon as you can. You're worth better. What's the point of working for a man you despise, who dislikes you? I'm afraid you're too closely associated with me for that to alter -

30

RICHARD: Thank you for my profile, Miss. Do I get to answer it or should I get my mother to come and see you?

VIVIEN: You asked.

RICHARD: Isn't it a little egotistical of you to assume that he will carry on this vendetta when you've gone? He'll simply turn you into a non-person. We won't mention your name. And... I don't care for your assumption that I only exist as a creature of your making - bobbing along in the wake of your massive personality.

VIVIEN: For goodness' sake, calm down and try to act rationally. You have been badly treated, but not by me - as a moment's thought should tell you.

RICHARD: Viv, will you stop being so bloody detached and analytical. The fact remains that between you, you've spiked my chances of promotion. What gives you the right to interfere? I resent you treating me like one of your uncooperative Sixth Formers, but I don't give a damn whether the motives were vindictive or altruistic. I am left precisely where I've always been. In the shit!

VIVIEN: Precisely! That's all there is here. I'm sorry if you resent it - but - I'm leaving a whole ugly mess of failure behind me. I have no pride in what I've done. I've kept the place going by doing the Head's dirty work for him. Covering up. Picking up the pieces. Keeping quiet when I shouldn't have done. Yes, and feeling secretly pleased when people said 'It's a pity Mrs Chadwick isn't the Headmistress. This school would be nothing without her.' I probably will be a non-person by September, but it isn't just a piece of monstrous egotism to say that things will be very different when I've gone. They will be a great deal worse. I should have gone years ago. I've let myself and everyone else down by doing such a brilliant job. It's a definition of corruption and I am not proud of it. I think too highly of you to want to see you go the same way. What do you want my job for?

RICHARD: The money. *(Pause)* Oh don't look embarrassed. The labourer is worthy of his hire! You can afford to have scruples and agonize about what you're doing. You've only got yourself to think about. We have an eight-month-old baby. Josie is no longer at work - which was the only way we could afford the blood-money on our lovely little house. Which is precisely the sort of house I was brought up in and my parents couldn't get out of fast enough. I'm hanging on to a few scruples about what we do to the kids, but anything else is a luxury and I can't afford it! *(Bitterly)* I came into this job with a burning idealism - I think - I can't remember - and a passionate love of literature, instilled into me by my lovely old English teacher. I wanted to pass that on to kids like me. I didn't realise it was a voluntary activity!

VIVIEN: Can the money be enough then?

RICHARD: Enough to pay my mortgage. The rest I can ignore. All right. All right. I believe you. Sorry I blew my top. But I don't think I've got anything to thank you for.

VIVIEN: You will.

RICHARD: You reckon? Just write me down as the light that you failed. Social engineering is a very inexact science. Lisa Stephenson is also for the chop.

VIVIEN: *(Startled)* Lisa? Why?

RICHARD: Rationalizing the situation. She's never here anyway. Her German and History teachers can't remember what she looks like.

VIVIEN: She's only the brightest child I've ever come across. And certainly in this school.

RICHARD: Pretty selective, though, isn't she? She only comes near the place after school for extra English lessons with you. What are the rest of us supposed to do? Send a taxi for her?

VIVIEN: She's exceptional -

RICHARD: You can say that again! Does she know you're going?

VIVIEN: No.

RICHARD: I thought not.

VIVIEN: I was going to tell her today... but she hadn't done some work I set her and I was annoyed. No. I took the opportunity to duck out of telling her. I can't see any answer... I'm going to be miles away. I've painted myself into a corner, but I'm - responsible for her. I talked her into staying on at school -

RICHARD: - in a manner of speaking -

VIVIEN: I persuaded her that she ought to go to University.

RICHARD: Will she make it?

VIVIEN: She's got a better brain than any of us. If she doesn't there's something badly wrong with the system.

RICHARD: Vivien, you've been in the system twenty years Haven't you noticed yet?

VIVIEN: She's a joy to teach. *(Smiling)* Give or take the odd spat.

RICHARD: She may be as bright as you say she is. She is also bright enough to be a manipulative, vicious-minded little bitch, who will take the greatest delight in leaving anyone in the shit, as long as it doesn't involve any effort.

VIVIEN: *(Briskly; with a hint of amusement)* Naturally, I disagree, but I'm sorry you see it like that. I was going to ask you to take over her extra tuition after I've gone.

RICHARD: Thank you very much. I'm adequate as a crammer for Lisa, but not as Head of Department. I suppose that's a kind of perverted compliment.

VIVIEN: *(Sharply)* It means I think you're a good teacher.

RICHARD: The answer, if you're really asking the question seriously, is no. And I'm not being petty. I disagree fundamentally with what you've done to Lisa.

VIVIEN: To?

RICHARD: To. And for. We shall have to wait and see how it turns out. I think you've done more harm than good singling her out. But that's your prerogative. I could be wrong. On a practical level there isn't a male teacher in the borough who would spend five minutes alone with her.

Vivien gives a little exclamation of disgusted impatience.

That's not sexist bias, or male fantasizing, it's an observable fact.

VIVIEN: Thank you. You were my last hope.

RICHARD: Here is a really revolutionary idea. Persuade her to come to school - and take her chance with everybody else.

VIVIEN: Of course that's the answer. But it's not going to happen, is it? I shall just have to wash my hands of her. Her mother will be pleased. I think I probably have a powerful enemy there.

RICHARD: Very likely. And little Lisa was down the pub the other night matching her mum gin for gin. Probably fella for fella as well.

VIVIEN: I've never met her mother.

RICHARD: How do you imagine her?

VIVIEN: *(Surprised)* I don't... well... like Lisa... I suppose - only beaten. She sounds pretty miserable from what Lisa says

RICHARD: She's about thirty-two, thirty-three. Looks twenty-five and she's gobsmackingly beautiful. Not just pretty. Stop and gape with your mouth open beautiful. Men and women. She trails into the pub, full of women who've bothered, wearing a terrible collection of old clothes - real rubbish not designer tat, usually half-cut. And stops the traffic. Sometimes she plasters her face with make-up... misses with most of it... but it doesn't matter. But underneath it all she's a very boring woman. And neurotic. Men don't bother with her two nights running. She's not very bright either. All she's got going for her is being beautiful. And all that's got her is Lisa and a drink problem.

VIVIEN: Poor girl.

RICHARD: Which one?

VIVIEN: 'Ignorance is a delicate fruit; touch it and the bloom is gone.' So you think I have made a pretty good job of insuring that instead of being an embittered, illiterate drunk, Lisa will manage to become an embittered, half-educated drunk?

RICHARD: We're just here to keep them quiet for a few years and get them their requisite worthless scraps of paper.

VIVIEN: This was an area of my life I thought I had reasonably under control. I'm beginning to feel I can't fight my way out of anything.

34

RICHARD: Cheer up. Things will look a lot worse by Friday.

VIVIEN: Do you think it would be a good idea if I wrote to Lisa?

RICHARD: Coward.

VIVIEN: And explained -

She stops. There is nothing to say. The lights fade on the scene. Richard goes out, Vivien remains on stage.

The scene changes to the cottage. The lights come up on Grace. With infinite care and great difficulty she attempts to get out of her wheelchair. It is obvious that although she has very little strength she has extreme tenacity and will-power. Eventually she manages to pull herself into a standing position. With all her weight on her left side she attempts to drag her right leg forward. Vivien moves towards her instinctively to take her arm. Grace snaps at her, annoyed that Vivien is making her waste her precious energy in speaking.

GRACE: No! Get away!! Leave me -

Vivien, undecided what to do for the best, hovers indecisively near her mother, ready to help.

GRACE: *(Snarling)* Go away!!

The 'phone rings. Vivien glances round and moves away reluctantly, towards the door.

I don't need any help...

Very painfully, and with the utmost difficulty, Grace attempts to walk. She manages a few steps away from the wheelchair, then like a baby, taking its first steps, she crumples and falls.

VIVIEN: Oh Christ!

She moves towards Grace and stands awkwardly over her.

Are you - all right?

GRACE: Of course I'm not. Get me back in that chair.

VIVIEN: No. Wait a minute. I don't know that I should move you. You might have broken something.

GRACE: For pity's sake, Vivien! Stop being such a fool. Your pathetic assumption of competence is the most irritating thing I have yet had to suffer - aahh!

She winces as Vivien tries to move her. Vivien is suddenly like an awkward, aggressive schoolgirl.

VIVIEN: *(Coldly)* Where does it hurt then?

GRACE: I don't know. I can't feel anything. Remember?

Allan comes in. He seizes up the situation and, very skilfully and gently, lifts Grace back into her chair.

ALLAN: Another suicide bid, Grace? You're not going to break much more than the odd hip hurling yourself down those steps.

He crosses to the sofa. There is a strong walking stick behind it.

When she makes these escape bids we generally give her this.

VIVIEN: *(With suppressed anger)* I didn't know. She didn't say -

ALLAN: You're wanted on the 'phone, Vivien. A Mr Shaw. Sounded very agitated.

Vivien goes out. Allan hands Grace her stick.

And why didn't you ask Vivien to give you this?

GRACE: It's nothing to do with Vivien. As she has made very clear. She is here to bring me grapes and look surreptitiously at her watch - not to concern herself with my problems.

ALLAN: I don't think we need mention this to Vera. She'd probably make too much of it.

GRACE: Thank you.

ALLAN: Your problems will be over when she gets back. Somebody told her that old Mrs Conway left a rusty Zimmer frame in her garden shed when she departed this life. So Mother is going to see if a bit of metal polish and a personalized number plate will make it suitable for you. Are you all right?

GRACE: Oh perfectly thank you.

Vivien returns, looking anxious.

VIVIEN: That was Richard Shaw. He's one of my colleagues.

Mother... Allan - Look, I'm afraid I shall have to go back. Now. There's been - there is - a problem and I'm the only person who can sort it out. I'm very sorry but I have no alternative. *(To Allan)* Will you thank Vera for me and tell her - that I had to go?... *(To Grace)* Are you - all right?

GRACE: Need you ask?

Vivien turns away. The lights come up on the study area. Lisa enters quietly with a letter in her hand. She stands looking at it.

GRACE: You'd better hurry. There's nothing to keep you here.

VIVIEN: I'll get back - if I can.

GRACE: Why bother? There's no need.

VIVIEN: Nevertheless.

GRACE: Nevertheless. You might as well go where you're - needed. I do apologize for encroaching on your valuable time.

VIVIEN: Goodbye mother. For the moment. Goodbye Allan.

She goes out.

ALLAN: Bad luck, Grace. You'll have to think of something else.

He goes out. Grace sits quite still, staring bleakly after Vivien. The lights slowly fade on her. Lisa looks up from the letter and stares unseeingly ahead of her. She speaks quite quietly and unemphaticallly, separating the words as if they bore no relation to each other.

LISA: 'Dear. - Lisa.'

The lights fade.

END OF ACT ONE

ACT TWO

Vivien's study has been vandalized - books pulled from the shelves, their pages ripped out and flung across the floor, and graffiti sprayed across the empty shelves. The desk has been pushed onto its side, the drawers hanging out. The metal waste paper basket has been stuffed full of papers and used as an incinerator. It has been set on the up-ended desk and bits of blackened and charred paper are spilling out of it. A large white envelope is propped up against it. Vivien is sitting dejectedly beside the desk. After a moment the door opens and Richard comes in. He looks at Vivien for a moment. She does not acknowledge his presence.

RICHARD: You haven't opened your letter.

Vivien stares at the envelope.

VIVIEN: No. *(Looking round the room)* Does anyone else know about this?

RICHARD: No. At least I presume not. Des was on duty when I came in on Saturday morning. I had my own keys - there's no need for him to come up here.

VIVIEN: *(Remotely)* Why didn't you tell Des - so that he could get the police in?

RICHARD: I'm not doing anything off my own bat. Can you imagine Himself's face if I got the cops in?

VIVIEN: You wouldn't have had to. It's the caretaker's job... security.

RICHARD: All right. So you go and tell Des then.

Vivien does not move or speak.

For Christ's sake, Viv, this is your room not mine. *(Deliberately)* I am deferring to my Head of Department....

As she still does not answer he softens his approach.

38

Look. You've... always protected your privacy in this little cubby-hole... I'm not doing anything else for your blue-eyed girl but I thought you might like to decide for yourself what to do about all this -

VIVIEN: You're assuming that Lisa did this?

RICHARD: Aren't you?

VIVIEN: Oh yes.

She picks up a book and holds it up by the cover. The pages are all torn and burnt. She lets them flip over slowly - what is left of them.

The Oxford Book of Seventeenth Century Verse. On India paper. 'Presented to Vivien Harper. For Excellence.' I lent it to Lisa.

RICHARD: I'm sorry.

VIVIEN: So am I... I feel... sick.

She leans down, picks up another shredded, blackened book, looks at it briefly and lets it drop.

I can't bear it when people destroy books... burn them... it's not the Nazis or... anything... Just -

She stops and sits staring, her eyes unfocused. When she speaks it is quietly, almost with difficulty, a wondering note in her voice, apparently trying not to cry.

I never throw books away... That's my problem now. Trying to find somewhere to live that will take all my books. Right back to the **Golden Wonder Book** I had when I was five... But everywhere's too small... or there are no shelves... *(With icy calm)* This is very embarrassing. I didn't cry when my Father died but I seem to be crying over the **Oxford Book of Seventeenth Century Verse**... very inappropriate...

She sits quite still. Her face a mask of misery, with tears running down her cheeks. After a moment Richard rather awkwardly hands her a neatly folded white handkerchief. She looks at it incredulously, her mood changing in a flash.

VIVIEN: Good God! Where did you get this from?

She dissolves into helpless laughter.

That is the most incongruous - from you!

RICHARD: *(With a grin)* My wife is a nicely-brought up, old-fashioned girl. I may be a shambling scruff on the surface but underneath I'm immaculate. You should see my underpants.

VIVIEN: No thank you. I can't promise to let you have this back in such a pristine state.

RICHARD: That's all right. I think Josie's making a rhetorical point about being stuck at home with the baby. What are you going to do about all this?

VIVIEN: I don't know. I don't know yet.

RICHARD: You've got to do something. You can't leave it like this, without saying anything.

VIVIEN: Is that why you 'phoned me?

RICHARD: Yes. I assumed you'd want to protect Lisa.

Vivien gets up, suddenly irritable.

VIVIEN: Yet another mess to clear up. I'm bloody useless at it actually... I ought to get my Auntie Vera onto this one. Are you suggesting we just clear up and say nothing

RICHARD: We? You. Or Lisa. I'm just a harmless bystander.

Vivien looks at him.

I'm so weak I'll probably give you a hand... If that's what you want?

VIVIEN: Thank you.

She picks up the letter and turns the envelope over, looking at it. It is very large.

'Mrs Chadwick. Private and personal. By hand.' Hm! That's Lisa's writing.

Very slowly she opens it. It is an enormous garishly coloured 'Good luck in your new job' card. Vivien stares at the front.

'We're crying 'cos we'll miss you so.'

She opens it slowly and after a pause, in a level voice empty of all emotion, she continues.

'But we know you've got to go.
Loadsa luck in your new job.'

She stands quite still. There is a long pause.

RICHARD: And?

VIVIEN: *(Neutrally)* She's put 'To Mrs Chadwick on the occasion of her leaving;
'Just for a handful of silver she left us;
Just for a riband to stick in her coat.'....
(Flatly, to herself) 'He'... it should be 'he'.

RICHARD: Eh?

VIVIEN: Browning. **The Lost Leader.** It's about Wordsworth...
(Carefully) Then underneath she's written: 'I hope you die of cancer, you fucking hypocrite.'

She lets the card fall to the floor and sits wearily, her elbow on the desk, her head resting on her hand. Richard picks up the card and looks at it.

RICHARD: Never read much Browning. The rest is -

VIVIEN: *(Without moving)* Shut up! The rest is - recognizable. Authentic. Only to be expected... I'm sorry. I shouldn't snap at you. I am sick of being self-controlled.

RICHARD: Yes. Well this little effusion might as well go the same way as all the rest.

He takes out his cigarette lighter and holding the card by one corner sets it alight. He tips the contents of the waste bin onto the floor and at the last moment lets the card drop into it.

VIVIEN: It's the one with 'never glad confident morning again' in.

She raises her head and watches the card burn. When she speaks again her voice is distant and unemphatic.

41

VIVIEN: 'We that had loved him so; followed him; honoured him,
Lived in his mild and magnificent eye;
Learned his great language, caught his clear accents,
Made him our pattern to live and to die,
Shakespeare was of us. Milton was for us.
Burns, Shelley were with us - they watch from their graves.
He alone breaks from the van and the freemen.
He alone sinks to the rear with the slaves!'

Richard watches her narrowly but does not say anything.

I recited it once in a poetry competition. I got third prize. It
was one of the things I put Lisa onto. I did a lot of that.
(Savagely) I enjoyed it... Showing off. Lots of cross
references... That's one of the little tricks to suggest width of
reading, and knowledge of poetry, outside the syllabus. Very
flattering of course to be treated like a student. Or perhaps I
felt flattered. Perhaps she didn't give a damn... She obviously
understood what I was driving at.

RICHARD: That bugs you more than her own little home-made
message, doesn't it?

VIVIEN: *(Bitterly)* Oh Browning puts the boot in more *tellingly* than
Lisa don't you think? *(Regaining her icy self command)* I'm
not very interested in her personal opinion of me. I am very
angry about what she has done here though. I wouldn't have
cared particularly if she'd vandalized my car.

RICHARD: *(Softly)* Liar.

VIVIEN: If you like. *(Getting up, briskly, in full control of herself)* I
have decided what I am going to do. Extremely unethical but
never mind. I'm going to clear all this up. You say Des hasn't
seen it. There is no need for anyone - other than you, me - and
Lisa - to know about it. I'm leaving. I don't want to be dragged
back, you certainly don't want to be bothered with all the fuss
everyone, especially the Head, would make. And there is no
reason why Lisa should have the satisfaction of any reaction
to what she's done. I have to clear out this room anyway.

RICHARD: And you'd rather no-one else had the satisfaction of
knowing Lisa had crapped all over you.

42

VIVIEN: Do you think ordinary paint-stripper will get that off?

Richard shrugs.

(Stiffly) Richard. Thank you. Very much. For keeping this quiet. Could you give me a hand clearing up? I want to get it done as quickly as possible. Then I can get out.

RICHARD: What if we get caught? You're leaving. I'm not.

VIVIEN: Oh. That was selfish of me. I'm sorry. You needn't worry. I'll do it. You might as well go and pretend you haven't seen it.

RICHARD: No. I'll help you. I suppose it was my fault for finding it.

VIVIEN: Thank you. I'll go and get some dustbin bags from Des. I'll tell him I'm clearing out my study. Taking all my things away.

She picks up her poetry book and drops it in the waste bin. Richard watches her then moves across and sets the desk to rights and pushes the drawers back in. Vivien continues to pick up the scattered papers and books. She looks round vaguely, realising it is a waste of time to pick them up with nowhere to put them. With a touch of embarrassment she puts them in a pile on the floor and gets up and begins to go out.

RICHARD: I'll go and get some paint-remover.

VIVIEN: *(With a little laugh)* Don't go to B&Q. Lisa may be there.

She goes out. Richard looks round.

RICHARD: *(With a sigh)* Browning. Stupid bitch.

*He goes out. The scene changes from the study to the cottage. Grace wheels herself in and sits still for a moment. She has a look almost of panic on her face as she looks round. Then she wheels herself across to the piano. There is a sheet of music open on the piano - Ravel's **Pavane For A Dead Infanta**. She begins to pick out a few notes with her left hand, very hesitantly, with the notes separated. She looks at the music more carefully and begins to play the left hand properly, which she does rather well. She is so absorbed in what she is doing that she does not see Allan enter quietly upstage. He stands watching her. After a while she lifts her right hand onto the keyboard and attempts to play the piece properly. But*

43

her right hand will not obey her and the result is distressing to her. She perseveres for a moment, then stops, staring bleakly at the piano.

ALLAN: Go on.

She looks up at him, startled.

GRACE: What for? It's fairly pointless isn't it? Murdering a favourite piece of music for the sake of some rather dubious therapy. I'd be better off with five-finger exercises.

Painfully, clumsily she plays five consecutive notes with her right hand. Allan smiles and moves across to her.

ALLAN: May I?

He moves her wheelchair away a little, so that he can sit on the piano stool.

I'll play the right hand.

He counts her in under his breath and begins to play the right hand. Grace joins in with the left. They play quite well, given the difficulties, becoming increasingly absorbed in what they are doing. Vera comes in, carrying a knitting bag. Grace stops playing immediately and moves very slightly away from the piano.

VERA: Oh! I wondered what on earth you were doing!

She takes Grace's wheelchair and moves her out of the way across the room. Allan swivels on the piano stool and watches ironically.

VERA: It is nice to see you at that piano again, Allan. Kettle's on! Do you want the TV, Grace?

GRACE: No.

Allan turns back to the piano and begins to play again, softly. He plays very well. Grace listens intently. Vera pulls a chair closer to her and speaks brightly as though to a child.

VERA: Now, dear, you can help me and yourself at the same time. You can hold this wool for me.

She produces several skeins of Aran wool.

VERA: You don't mind, do you? It's a nuisance, I know. She'd got a lot of wool already in balls but this was the only pure wool. I don't like all these acrylics. That's all you can get these days, especially out here. And it'll exercise your hand a bit. All right?

Grace holds out her hands obediently. Vera alters the position of her right hand rather roughly and drapes the wool over it. She then begins to wind the wool from Grace's hands.

No. Come on. Not just your left hand. We've got to get some movement back in that right hand. You've got more grip than that.

Grace closes her eyes and allows Vera to wind the wool. She flexes her hands obediently, but as she is taking no notice of what Vera is doing or where the wool is going, the operation does not proceed as smoothly as it should. The tension mounts between the two women.

Just a minute. Keep still.

She bends forward to untangle the strands.

You never were much of a one for handiwork were you? I remember that chairback you made for Mummy in Needlework lessons. Drawn threadwork and sweet peas embroidered on it, it was supposed to have. Lots of little holes where you'd had to unpick it. And bloodstains. That's what it consisted of when you got it home. And it was black as the ace of spades. Mummy did laugh.

Vera laughs none too kindly. Grace does not respond. Allan continues to play softly.

That's a bit droning, Allan. It's lovely hearing you play but let's have something a bit cheerful.

*Allan looks across at her then with great delicacy and a cheerful lilt, plays Chopin's **Funeral March**.*

(With a laugh) Allan! Really!

45

*He begins to play **Wiener Blut**.*

VERA: That's better.

> *Pause. Allan plays and the two women sit winding the wool.*

GRACE: *(Harshly)* What an idyllic little scene. All we lack is the crackling apple-log fire.

VERA: Oh, it's not cold enough for a fire. Do you want a rug? Are you feeling chilly?

GRACE: No. I'm all right.

> *She lets her hands drop.*

VERA: Hands up!

> *Grace sweeps her hands up sharply. The left hand goes higher than the right and some of the strands come adrift from her right hand.*

Honestly Grace. I really do think the rocking chair would make a better job of this wool. I've got another seventeen skeins, you know! I can see I'm going to get this cardigan finished by the turn of the century at this rate.

> *Allan stops playing.*

ALLAN: Do you want me to lend a hand?

VERA: No don't you bother. I was doing this for Grace's benefit. I thought we could help each other. But obviously I was wrong.

GRACE: You will have noticed I have not uttered a single word of complaint. Come on, do your worst, Vera. Let's sit here till we've done all eighteen

> *She thrusts her hands out towards Vera with an aggressive lunge. The wool comes off her right hand. She struggles to get it back. With a little snap of triumph Vera reaches over and rather roughly puts it back on her hands. She continues winding the wool, very fast now.*

VERA: Play that one I like, dear.

ALLAN: *(Drily)* Yes of course.

> *He looks at her quizzically. There is a pause.*

ALLAN: You hum it and I'll play it, lady.

VERA: Oh you know - ...

She hums, rather inaccurately, **Bells Across The Meadow.**

GRACE: *(Through gritted teeth)* Dear God!

VERA: What's that?

GRACE: Nothing.

Allan, with only a hint of irony, plays **Bells Across The Meadow.**

VERA: That was always Mummy's favourite.

ALLAN: *(Under his breath)* Kept her quiet when she was having one of her turns.

GRACE: Is that why I am being subjected to it now?

ALLAN: *(With a grin)* Sorry!

VERA: *(With an odd little air of triumph)* There's no need to be rude, Grace. I thought you were supposed to be musical. Oh, I know, it's not highbrow enough for you. But I think Allan plays beautifully. He always has. He could have made a career of it if he'd wanted to. I don't think it befits people who can't do anything themselves to sit and sneer at those who can. I think it's very nice of Allan to give up his time to amusing you - us. I mean. Vivien isn't the only one who has a busy life to run. Elsewhere. Nobody is going to pretend it's easy fitting everything in. I know she has a lot to do and there was nothing she could do about it. I'm sure we're all as upset as you are that she had to go running back as soon as she got here... She hasn't 'phoned yet, I suppose?

Allan gets up from the piano.

ALLAN: I think I'll go and make us all a nice cup of tea.

He goes out quickly.

VERA: I wish you'd make a bit of an effort, Grace. You know how he hates scenes. Oh! I must keep an eye on the time. My Gardening Programme's on at half-past. I don't like to miss it. It's conifers and heathers this week - Do you want to see it?

47

GRACE: If you like.

VERA: No. If you like. You must try, Grace, you won't get better if you don't help yourself. If you just sit there and - feel sorry for yourself, it'll take twice as long. Look at old Mrs Freeman - she's crippled with arthritis. She doesn't sit around moping. She gets herself out, and - if it takes her all morning - she gets down to the Post Office and back to collect her pension. And she hasn't got a brain in her head. She never has had.

Grace gives a bark of unamused laughter.

GRACE: Perhaps I'm over-qualified to do two hundred and fifty yards in an hour and a half.

VERA: You and Vivien are both the same. Too much thinking and not enough thought.

Grace looks at her curiously.

GRACE: I could wish you didn't resent me so much.

VERA: That's exactly what I mean. I don't resent anybody or anything. I'm too busy for one thing.

Allan returns with a tray of tea.

VERA: Oh! That's nice. Thank you, dear.

ALLAN: Yes. It was only an excuse of course, but having fled into the kitchen I had to do something.

With his usual slightly exaggerated courtesy to Grace he clears a space beside her, takes the wool off her hands and lays it gently down in her lap, and hands her a cup of tea. Grace reaches out for it with her right hand.

VERA: *(Sharply)* Use your other hand. We don't want a repetition of last night.

With a clumsily defiant gesture, Grace lifts the tea with her right hand. Her hand turns over with the weight and she tips the contents of the cup into her lap. There is a pause. Vera sighs.

VERA: Why will you never be told?

GRACE: This - is - scalding - me.

Vera lifts the sodden skein of wool from her lap.

VERA: Oh, thank you! Thank you very much. Take her into the kitchen, Allan. I'll see to her in there. I suppose I'd better go and get a towel. You might as well get into your night things, Grace. There's no point in getting dressed again now. You're not going anywhere.

She glances at her watch.

Hm! Half-past. You do it on purpose, don't you?

She goes out. Allan goes to move the wheelchair but Grace stops him with a gesture.

GRACE: No. I can see to myself. Will you get me out of the front door, though. Please?

ALLAN: No. *(Pause)* Nor the back one either.

Grace looks at him contemptuously.

GRACE: You'll do anything for me, won't you? Except what I really want.

ALLAN: My dear Aunt Grace, for an intelligent woman you are shatteringly muddle-headed sometimes. You are so much brighter than my poor dear Mother. Why do you go out of your way to give her the upper hand? She'll get it anyway, so why let her revel in her little victories?

GRACE: How long are you staying?

Allan shrugs.

What have you come for?

ALLAN: *(With a grin)* To shine of course in contrast to my thoughtless cousin, Vivien.

GRACE: Not very difficult.

She wheels herself out. Allan moves to open the door for her and guide her chair through the narrow doorway.

GRACE: Thank you.

ALLAN: A pleasure.

He turns back into the room and sits at the piano. He

49

plays - right hand only - the opening phrase of the Ravel. Then stops abruptly in mid-phrase and remains motionless.

The lights fade on him and the scene changes to Vivien's study. The graffiti have gone; the desk is upright, with the battered pot plants lying on top of it. Round the desk there are several cardboard boxes of books standing on the floor, as well as four or five bulging dustbin bags, neatly tied at the top, stacked by the door. The room is now characterless and rather desolate. The pictures are piled up by the desk; the posters, rolled in cardboard tubes, are in boxes; the broken glass cleared away.
Vivien and Richard enter. He is carrying a large plastic bag of potting compost. Vivien has a watering-can, a small trowel, and two or three flower-pots. She crosses and sets them down on the desk and begins to pick over the sorry-looking plants. Richard morosely sets down the compost. Vivien tears it open and begins to re-pot the plants.

RICHARD: This is a ludicrous waste of time.

VIVIEN: *(Coldly)* Please go then. There's no need -

She stops. There is a pause.

RICHARD: Why don't you just throw them away?

VIVIEN: No. They're not dead. I am going to salvage as much as I can.

RICHARD: You've done that already. The room's in better shape then it was before you took it over.

VIVIEN: Good. Thank you for all your help.

RICHARD: That's all right - I just feel rather a fool - the clandestine nature of the whole operation. This is the most undignified - not to say ridiculous way for two mature members of the NUT to behave. It's probably actionable as well.

VIVIEN: I am not giving that child the satisfaction of making a fuss about it.

RICHARD: 'That child.'

VIVIEN: *(Biting her lip)* Yes all right. I am angry. I am - hurt. Let down. I'm feeling pretty petty... And it's all my fault, isn't it? I picked out a little - guttersnipe - and tried to change her life. Very presumptuous. Meddling, interfering, insensitive, bone-headed *do-gooder.* Using her to make me feel good. I've got what I deserve, haven't I? I suppose I expected her to know the rules - to behave like a nice, well-mannered, *(With loathing)* grateful little middle-class miss with just a few working-class rough edges that exposure to my superior culture could smooth away! It won't do her any good to be charged with criminal damage will it? *(With a little laugh of self disgust)* She's pretty damaged already isn't she?... And I - have done my best to... damage her even further. And I don't want the humiliation.

RICHARD: End of story.

VIVIEN: End of experiment. Once I've cleared out of here I'll stick rigidly to the rules.

> *She is rigid with tension.*

RICHARD: *(Cynically)* And you don't even want to get back at her?

VIVIEN: Of course I do! That would be even more humiliating... *(With quiet bitterness)* I'm no sodding good at people, that's my trouble! I've got all the right ideas - wonderfully perceptive about characters in books - I don't miss a nuance! *(Brightly)* I don't know why I'm making such a fuss. All teachers have their failures, don't they? I know why she did it but I wish she hadn't done it to me. But then that's only pride. I couldn't face Mrs Parker saying, 'I told you so!' So I'll just leave this room completely blank. Wiped clean. No trace of me - or anybody else. Let's face it, by half term everybody will have forgotten me. And if Lisa doesn't turn up everyone will breathe a collective sigh of relief. After all, it doesn't rate very high on the scale of atrocities, does it? Burning a few books. Not compared with knifings in the playground and drug-pushers at the gates. *(With a little laugh)* I've been pushing the really dangerous drugs haven't I?

RICHARD: Don't flatter yourself. It ain't dangerous if they don't want it!

As Vivien finishes reclaiming each plant, she places it carefully into a shallow cardboard box beside the desk. The contents of the room are now stacked or packed away neatly round the desk or by the door. Richard looks round thoughtfully

RICHARD: I wonder if the new Head of English will want this room.

VIVIEN: Depends how gregarious she - he - is. My chief requirement was always to be as far away from the Staff-Room as possible.

She too looks round the room, rather ruefully.

RICHARD: Pangs?

VIVIEN: Some. I've been here eleven years.

RICHARD: About time you moved on. I don't like Schoolteachers who stick around. There are only two people on this Staff I can stand spending more than five minutes with. You're both women. And Alison Finch looks too much like Michele Pfeiffer for a respectable married man to say more than Hello to. Especially if those sewer-rat Fourth years are around. They didn't make Maths Teachers like that in my day - and they certainly didn't let them loose on adolescent boys.

Vivien is hardly listening to him. She is mechanically sweeping her hand across the desk. She has collected a small amount of spilled compost. She begins to brush it off the desk into her cupped hand. Richard crosses and catches hold of her wrist.

RICHARD: Leave it.

VIVIEN: Don't be silly. I'm only clearing up. Let go of my wrist please.

Richard turns her wrist over. She automatically closes her hand, then as he does not release her wrist, she opens her hand and lets it go limp. The compost spills onto the floor.

VIVIEN: This is ridiculous.

RICHARD: Exactly. This isn't your room any more. The cleaners will dust and sweep it before term begins.

Vivien sits down rather wearily and begins to fiddle with

the books on her desk, putting them in neater piles.

RICHARD: Stop it. You're becoming obsessional.

VIVIEN: Old maidish. I've probably been a widow too long. They're supposed to be merry aren't they?

RICHARD: Yeah. But school teachers aren't.

VIVIEN: I just want to walk away from here and leave no trace of myself behind. I don't want anyone to find anything - a book, or a postcard, or a scribbled note - so they can say, 'Oh, that's what she was like.'

RICHARD: Just as well Lisa won't be back then isn't it?

She stares at him wonderingly.

VIVIEN: Why did you 'phone me?

RICHARD: It was - your business. You were the one to sort it out.

VIVIEN: Why did you help me?

RICHARD: I was seriously tempted to close the door and leave it for someone else to find.

VIVIEN: Why didn't you? It would have demonstrated very neatly the destructive folly of my meddling. And Lisa's - unsuitability. After the way - you think - I treated you.

RICHARD: I'm not a neurotic. I get mad. I don't get even. I'm not interested in kicking you when you're down.

VIVIEN: How did you find it? What were you doing here?

RICHARD: Oh. Invading your privacy, of course...

VIVIEN: I'm sorry. I didn't mean that.

RICHARD: The window was open. There was a cardboard box wedging it open, with a message scrawled on it. I don't propose to tell you what it said. I wasn't just thinking of you. It mentioned me as well.

VIVIEN: I see.

Richard gestures towards the boxes of books on the desk.

RICHARD: Do you want all these put in your car? Now it's all sorted you may as well take them home.

VIVIEN: Yes. I might as well... Add them to the general chaos. I've sold my flat... All my possessions are piled high in cardboard boxes waiting to move on. I dislike clutter. That's probably why I haven't found anywhere I want to move to. Can't find the right sterile environment.

RICHARD: Here's an essay title for you. A Level. 'Does the puréed spinach on page 65 of **Mansfield Park,** spat out by Toby Shaw, while his distracted parent was feeding him with one hand and marking essays with the other, represent a cosy domestic fantasy or a necessary intrusion of reality into the hothouse atmosphere of the novel?'

VIVIEN: *(Wincing)* I think it's a comforting cliché that only those with children really understand human relationships.

RICHARD: So do I. But everybody ought to recognize the element of sheer messiness. It's flung in your face when you've got kids.

VIVIEN: Thank you. For the help and the lesson. I'm not going to blame myself for this. Not entirely. People have to take some responsibility for their own actions.

RICHARD: You still call the tune, eh? If you always define the limits of every encounter so strictly you're bound to finish up with a vandalized room.

VIVIEN: What are you talking about?

RICHARD: Oh, come on, Viv, you're not a fool. When people come up against your ice barriers they're going to take an ice-pick to them.

Vivien looks away from him.

Talk about teaching by example rather than precept. I didn't fully grasp the difference between uninterested and disinterested till I met you.

Vivien sweeps some of the loose compost into a rubbish bag and then brushes her hands together to clean them.

VIVIEN: It's open season on me at the moment, is it?

RICHARD: *(Mockingly)* No. I like you. I respect you. I enjoy talking to you. Especially since Josie's abandoned brain for instinct -

even if it is temporary. Please God it is! I admire your calm efficiency in dealing with problems and cutting out the crap and getting things done. You'll make a lovely Head.

VIVIEN: But?

RICHARD: Oh forget it. It's presumptuous.

VIVIEN: And what you've said so far isn't?

RICHARD: You always slam the brakes on if anyone oversteps your limits. You don't get your hands dirty do you? Snow Queen.

> *The door opens suddenly and Lisa enters suspiciously fast. She is carrying a carrier bag with a few books and files in. She stands cool and at ease in the doorway.*

RICHARD: Good God!

VIVIEN: Enter Kai - or is it Gerda?

RICHARD: What are you doing here?

LISA: It's Monday. I always have my lesson with Mrs Chadwick on a Monday.

RICHARD: It is also the holidays.

LISA: Is it? Oh well, I got that wrong as well then didn't I?

> *She looks round the room speculatively.*

Oh, are you clearing your things out, Mrs Chadwick? I could have given you a hand. If you'd like. It's a bit late now though isn't it?

RICHARD: Just what do you think you're playing at, Lisa? Have you come to gloat? Check up on how much damage you've done? Talk about a dog returning to his vomit.

LISA: Bitch. Shouldn't you say bitch. If you mean me.

VIVIEN: *(To herself)* 'As a dog returneth to his vomit so a fool returneth to his folly.'

LISA: Pardon? I just came to return these books. *(Pause)* I think most of them are Library books. But one or two are yours.

RICHARD: What's the matter? Wouldn't they catch fire before? Slosh on a bit of paraffin this time. Or meths. I'm sure you've got plenty of that at home.

Lisa stares stonily at him.

VIVIEN: For God's sake, Richard. She's only a child!

She turns away and goes over to the window, standing with her back to them.

LISA: What's up? Has something been going on here?

VIVIEN: Don't pretend. You know perfectly well what you've done.

RICHARD: Fortunately your little fires didn't spread. Were you just after a limited strike or did you want to incinerate the whole school?

LISA: I don't know what you're talking about. I haven't done anything.

RICHARD: No, of course you haven't. But just out of scientific interest how and when did you get in here and vandalize this room?

LISA: What? No! Has this room be done over then? When? Wait a minute. Do you think I did it? That's awful of you.

VIVIEN: *(Half to herself)* Don't be tiresome, Lisa.

RICHARD: You didn't send any personalized Farewell cards either?

VIVIEN: Richard!

LISA: Cards? Me? No.

She stares coldly at Vivien.

LISA: I was going to get some flowers. I don't know anything about cards.

RICHARD: Come on. It was your handwriting -

LISA: Not mine. Let's have a look.

RICHARD: Ah. Yes. I er - It was burnt, like any other bit of anonymous filth.

Lisa smiles broadly at him.

LISA: Burnt it did you? That's a shame. I could have told you if it was my writing or not

RICHARD: Don't be insolent. You're lucky not to find yourself in court over this.

LISA: Over what? Doesn't look very vandalized to me. And you say there's a bit of non-existent evidence as well. What do you reckon they'd charge me with?

VIVIEN: *(Irritated)* Leave it. Both of you. The incident is closed.

> *There is a long pause. Vivien, by the window, is apparently lost in thought. Lisa is standing by the desk, quite self-contained, her carrier-bag clasped in her arms. Richard looks from one to the other. He is half angry half amused by Vivien's bracketing him with Lisa.*

RICHARD: I'll leave you then. Will there be anything else - *Mrs Chadwick?*

VIVIEN: *(Realising)* No... Richard, I - thank you. Very much. You know, I didn't mean to -

RICHARD: No. I know. Excuse me then. I've got messes of my own to go to.

> *Vivien holds out her hand rather desolately.*

VIVIEN: Goodbye. Thank you...very much. I'll see you ?

> *She stops.*

RICHARD: Possibly. If unlikely. Good luck.

> *He goes out.*

LISA: What a tosser! *(Pause)* Is he your toyboy?

VIVIEN: *(Icily)* If you could put the books down on the desk I'll see to them.

> *Pause.*

LISA: I want a word with you.

VIVIEN: Do you indeed? And do you have any reason to suppose that I want a word with you?

LISA: What did you think when you came in here? *(Pause)* You were a bit silly to let loverboy clear away the evidence weren't you? *(Pause)* Did you like the card? I chose it specially. They're a bit naff usually. The words. But I thought the verse was lovely. My Mum always likes the ones with the nice verses in. She gets quite upset if I get her one of those good taste cards with a nice restrained picture and fuck-all inside. Blank for your own message. Oh! I shouldn't swear, should I? What will you think of me? But you can't do anything about it can you? You're not my teacher any more. You've left. So have I. But don't tell anybody will you? I don't want them to know. *(Viciously)* I just want them to find out. When it's too fucking late. Perhaps I could write them a letter. I really appreciated your letter. You explained it all really well. Why you had to go. How sorry you were not to see me through to the next stage in my studies - wasn't that how you put it? Bit of a cliché perhaps? Do you know what I did with it? I wiped my arse with it.

> *She is near to angry tears. Vivien's refusal to respond has driven her almost out of control.*

VIVIEN: Oh my God. This is unnecessary.

LISA: I've brought these books back. Shall I put them straight in here?

> *She pulls open one of the rubbish sacks and drops the books inside.*

I brought you my essays as well. Do you want them or shall I just junk them now? I won't be needing them will I?

> *She has taken out a file of essays and is pulling the pages out and slamming them down on the desk.*

Here we are. 'Who gives a toss about T.S.Eliot?'; 'Wordsworth, poetic genius or sister-fucker?'; Prac. Crit. Prat Crap! Oh. There's the story I was telling you about.

> *She tears it to shreds.*

That's the best thing to do with that isn't it?

> *She throws the pieces of torn paper down and stamps on them, grinding them into the floor with her foot. She is out of control. A child having a tantrum. Vivien very deliberately slaps her face hard. Lisa stops, surprised. The two women stare at one another.*

LISA: What did you do that for? Nobody hits me. That's assault.

VIVIEN: You are hysterical. There are to be no more tantrums in here.

LISA: And you wanted to hit me anyway.

Vivien continues to look at her unwaveringly.

Because of what I did to your room. Your books.

Again there is no response from Vivien. Lisa continues, almost whining.

I'll get you another one... Some more... your own books I mean. Doesn't matter about the school books... That's what I came for really. I was going to get you your books and put them back. But I haven't got any money yet. *(Breaking down)* I'm sorry. I shouldn't have done it. But I do anything when I'm in a temper. Please say something to me. Please. I'm sorry.

VIVIEN: *(Slowly)* I honestly don't know what to say. Pick up those bits of paper.

Lisa begins to do so.

VIVIEN: Was that your only copy?

LISA: Yes.

VIVIEN: Silly girl. You'd better keep the bits then. Sit down.

Lisa does so. Vivien leans against the desk, half-sitting on the edge. She does not look at Lisa.

VIVIEN: *(Carefully choosing her words)* I... am sorry too. It was - cruel and - cowardly of me not to warn you that I was leaving. And it was a disastrous cop-out to send you that letter. You did the right thing with it.

LISA: *(Muttering)* I didn't -

VIVIEN: You should have done.

LISA: I didn't think you'd be like all the others. 'Dear Lisa you are now a nuisance. Get lost.'

VIVIEN: *(Wincing)* Yes. Prettily expressed over a page and a half that's what it was. Only it wasn't meant to be. To put it brutally you weren't at the top of my list of priorities. I was worried about you but I couldn't see any solution. So I took the coward's way out. *(Bitterly)* That's how I deal with all my problems now. You're not the only one. My mother is a problem. She's had a stroke and I'm leaving her to be looked after by - someone she detests. She's in a wheelchair so she can't express her feelings by smashing up my room. But I should have known better. At your age you are the first and only. Other people don't have problems... No that's unfair. We're all like that really. We just hide it a bit better.

LISA*:* *(With a kind of pride)* I've always been a problem. Right from the start. I could read when I started school. My Gran used to teach me words in her magazines. I always thought it was all dead easy at school. I couldn't understand why all the other kids couldn't understand... couldn't do things I could. They used to get their own back though when my mum turned up at half-past three pissed out of her brain. The teachers always talked about me behind their hands. 'Such a bright little girl. But so difficult. Dreadful home background.' They kept examining me to see if she'd been hitting me. I used to pretend she'd got this very rare illness that made her look as if she was drunk. I used to say she'd only live six months. By the time I got to the Middle School they were all saying 'Your Mum ain't dead yet, is she? Dead drunk more like.' *(Unemotionally)* They'd have put me in care if it hadn't been for Gran. She wouldn't speak to my Mum but she looked after me all right. Then she got married again and went to live in Reading. I suppose you know all this... From my files.

VIVIEN: Only the facts.

LISA: I do wish I was thick sometimes. My Mum's really thick, but I suppose it hasn't helped her much. And she's really pretty as well. She'll go off with anybody... *(Sardonically)* I've had more 'uncles' than you've had A-Level passes. I suppose I mucked up her life as well... She was only fifteen when she had me. I'm only here because she was too thick to have an abortion.

She looks at Vivien to see what effect this has had. Vivien looks stricken.

60

LISA: Are you feeling really sorry for me now? Most people do when I say that to them.

VIVIEN: Do you do that often?

LISA: Yes. When I want something. Or when I want to make people feel really bad. It would be much easier if I was a nice stupid little victim. Then all the nice people could help me. Get me a job as a hairdresser. Most people are as thick as pigshit. They just like to patronise you. I thought you were different. You didn't seem to think I was a problem. When I was in the First Year and I wrote those poems. And you told me to stay behind at break. I thought 'Oh God, here we go' 'Lisa, my dear, we all know your mum's a piss-head who screws around so if you have any problems don't hesitate to come to me and I'll have a good old wank about it.' But you -

She stops suddenly as if unable to continue. Vivien watches her narrowly.

It's all finished isn't it? It doesn't matter....

She moves restlessly about the room.

You were the only person made me feel important. You just said, 'These are very good poems, Lisa' and I was waiting for the rest and you didn't say it. For six years you never said it. 'This is very good work - it's such a *pity...*' You weren't bothered about me. You just treated me like an equal -

Vivien puts out her hand towards Lisa then draws it back as Lisa winces involuntarily.

VIVIEN: *(With difficulty)* My - admittedly studied - impulse is to... comfort you, but after six years of indifference that is obviously impossible. I'm glad I did something right if only by default.

LISA: The others used to wind me up about being your favourite. But most of them liked you so that just made it better. They know you don't - didn't - bullshit so that made it even better for me. If *you* thought I was any good I must be. It was only the other teachers I had any trouble with.

VIVIEN: Oh child - why - if only for self-interest - didn't you put your

61

head down and do enough work to keep them happy?

LISA: I haven't got any self-preservation. I don't know what's good for me. Anyway they're all just bastards.

VIVIEN: Even Richard Shaw?

LISA: He's all right. He might be better if I hadn't had you. He's a bit too keen to show you how brilliant he is.

VIVIEN: And you think I'm not?

LISA: I told you - I thought you were different. But it was all a con like everything else wasn't it? You're leaving. So am I. Thanks for nothing.

VIVIEN: Don't be such a self-dramatizing little fool. You're just going to walk out are you? What for? For revenge? It won't hurt me. So why try to hurt yourself? You've been hurt enough already. Look at it from the other angle. You've had six years of feeling important. That's not why I did it, but never mind. Perhaps it made me feel important too. You are cursed with a remarkable intellect and you write beautifully. You haven't a great deal to say yet but you have the beginnings of an individual voice, which is rare at your age. The interesting thing about you is not your much cherished, appalling background - and there are worse - but the fact that you are a uniquely gifted human being.

LISA: *(Ironically)* We're all uniquely gifted, Mrs Chadwick.

VIVIEN: Oh yes, I know. But some are more gifted than others. I wasn't concerned with your problems. There was nothing I could do about them. But the excitement - the development of your mind became - a passion.

LISA: Turned you on did it? Snatching me from the fire? Getting me away from all those morons who think school's a waste of time and teachers are a waste of air? Am I supposed to be grateful? You didn't give Michelle any private lessons because she can't read did you?

VIVIEN: *(Flatly)* Yes.

LISA: Oh. Well. Anyway. That doesn't matter.
'You taught me language and my profit on't

62

Is I know how to curse. The red plague rid you
For learning me your language.'

VIVIEN: *(Ruefully)* 'Hagseed hence!'

LISA: *(With a quick grin)* No. Hag is the one thing you can't call my mother. That's what I'll do though. Copy her. Chuck away the books and take to the bottle. And men. It should be an interesting little exercise. I wonder which I'll get first. Pregnant or Aids.

VIVIEN: *(Acidly)* It seems to me that psychological trauma has taken the place of Fate. No-one is allowed any free will any more. I know it's unfashionable but is there no possibility of using your brain - which you have learned how to use very precisely - to regulate your actions and make something of your life?

LISA: Is that what you did?

VIVIEN: *(Ruefully)* Not very successfully. That's the reason why I treated you so ham-fistedly. Not a lofty disregard for your troubles. You can only go so far - using your intellect to paper over the cracks. But you *can* go so far... Because I have - ultimately - let you down don't let it destroy everything else. Don't - I beg you - don't hurt yourself even more. *(With a half smile)* You've vandalized my study and burnt my books. Made your gesture. Let's say that puts an end - I've got the point.

LISA: This is all academic isn't it? Easy to say.

VIVIEN: Unlike you, I had a very smooth path. A little low on affection but you can't have everything. I was a clever girl too. But *my* mother gave me away. For the best possible motives. My father was a missionary and they thought I would be best off in a settled environment. So while they set off round the world I was left at home. Going to school. Winning all the prizes and being brought up by my Aunt who didn't like me much. But who did her Christian duty. And hated everything I cared for because she didn't understand it. You love your mother don't you?

LISA: *(Disturbed)* Yes. Yes I do. She's a stupid cow. She's really... beautiful, you know. She'd have been a lot better off without a

63

snotty kid around. But she thinks I'm brilliant. She'd love to go round saying, 'My Lisa's got into Oxford University. I don't know where she gets her brains from. Not me.' But she'd just as soon I didn't actually go.

VIVIEN: And your father?

LISA: Christ knows who he is. I don't think she knows but she thinks he must have been one of the clever ones.

VIVIEN: My father was the only one my mother cared tuppence about. She's the sort of woman I like. Whose company I enjoy. But she's ill now. And I haven't any room for her... Are you going to devote yourself to your mother

LISA: No.

VIVIEN: Good... I seem to be preaching a doctrine of total selfishness don't I? I don't think that's what I mean. It's never easy... I was a brilliant child. Look at me now. There are always more gifted children than gifted adults. Just give it a go and see what you can do. On your own. You'll make a lot of mistakes. I hope you don't make as many as I have.

LISA: I never intend to make any. I just can't help it.

VIVIEN: No. I know...

She chooses her words carefully, unsure how she will react herself to what she is about to say.

I want to tell you something. There are only two people who ever knew this. And one of them is dead. I got married the moment I came down from University. I'd known Angus for eighteen months. Two weeks before the wedding I discovered I was pregnant. It wasn't a problem. Angus had a job. So had I. We were getting married anyway. I was twenty. He was twenty four. I had an abortion. We didn't want a baby just then. We both had so much we wanted to do. We were young and healthy. There was plenty of time. Then Angus got leukaemia and died at twenty seven.

Lisa's face becomes a blank mask. It as if she wants to distance herself from Vivien's revelation.

LISA: Why did you tell me?

VIVIEN: As a warning? Or an explanation...

LISA: It's different each time round though isn't it?... Aren't you worried I'll tell people?

VIVIEN: It won't matter. It was - someone else. And... I won't be here.

LISA: *(Looking bleakly at her)* No.

VIVIEN: *(Suddenly brisk)* There is of course a simple, practical solution. When I have found myself somewhere to live and I've established myself in my new school we could continue with our lessons. In spite of... I shall only be twenty odd miles away. But you wouldn't come would you?

LISA: No... I might mean to -

VIVIEN: You don't need me any more you know.

LISA: Shouldn't that be the other way round?... Have you got my address - from the Office?

VIVIEN: I think so... But I can get it -

Lisa takes a sheet of paper from her file.

LISA: Here. Here it is. In case you forget.

Vivien takes the paper. She holds her hand out towards Lisa.

VIVIEN: Lisa -

But Lisa ignores her outstretched hand.

LISA: *(Looking down)* Goodbye. Thank you. I'll write to you. If you tell me where you are.

VIVIEN: Yes. Yes of course.

Pause.

LISA: I'm sorry I spoilt your book,

VIVIEN: It doesn't matter.

LISA: Yes it does... I liked it better when you ripped me up. This is embarrassing.

VIVIEN: Ripping you up didn't work either did it?

LISA: Worked better than you leaving.

VIVIEN: All right. Take a leaf out of my book. Just think about yourself. Work hard. Get away from here. Use your brains. Enjoy yourself.

LISA: Shut up! You don't believe any of that crap. What's University anyway? Just somewhere I can sod things up on a more intellectual scale. I mean it though. Thank you for all you've done for me. It does matter...

> *Her bravado breaks down and she speaks with painful intensity.*

But it should have been *me* that went away. Not you!!!

> *She runs out. Vivien stands looking at the piece of paper Lisa has given her. Then she crosses to the door, takes her coat, puts the paper in her pocket and goes out slamming the door. The lights fade as she goes.*

> *The scene changes to the cottage. Allan is sitting at the piano, idly picking out a few notes of* **Ma Mere L'Oye.** *He is lost in thought. Vivien comes in, with her coat on.*

ALLAN: Vivien! And we're fresh out of fatted calf.

VIVIEN: Hello.

ALLAN: The old dears have gone down to the village in an outburst of sisterly harmony. No. I tell a lie. Vera was being sisterly. Grace was - recalcitrant.

VIVIEN: You do surprise me.

> *She sits down, rather wearily, on the bed-settee, without taking her coat off.*

You're still here. I have to sleep on this monstrosity again.

> *Allan smiles.*

ALLAN: Have you solved your little problem?

VIVIEN: No. I've probably made it worse. *(Pause)* Somebody had broken into my study and vandalized it. Very petty. Nothing to make a fuss about. There's a break-in every holiday.

ALLAN: The disaffected striking back?

VIVIEN: I expect so.

66

ALLAN: And your presence was needed?

Vivien does not answer.

I expect you'll get a lot more of that sort of thing at your new school

VIVIEN: Probably. *(Savagely)* And I expect I've been promoted beyond my competence level so I'll leave a trail of disaffected disaster wherever I go.

ALLAN: You are like dear old Uncle Andrew. All this missionary zeal. Taking the true word to the poor benighted heathen. Why not just let the poor bloody heathen alone. They're quite happy with their funny little ways. Human sacrifice and satellite television.

VIVIEN: Oh shut up, Allan. I am absolutely pissed off with my life at the moment so if you keep on I shall either club you to death with that doorstop or have a fit of screaming hysterics.

She gets up and begins to go.

ALLAN: Don't go. I wanted a word with you. On your own

VIVIEN: Oh God. You certainly pick your moments. Go on. But I warn you if you have any problems I shall be seriously unsympathetic. 'When sorrows come, they come not single spies but in battalions.'

ALLAN: It's not a problem, More a business proposition.

Vivien is surprised.

ALLAN: *(Abruptly)* Has Grace made a will?

VIVIEN: I presume so. I've never asked her and she has never said anything to me.

ALLAN: Vera has of course. I am - naturally - the sole beneficiary.

VIVIEN: And?

ALLAN: Just about the most stupid thing grandmother Bailey did before she went completely gaga - at least I presume it was before - was to leave this house jointly to Grace and Vera. It was pretty convenient for Grace, of course. It meant she could justify dumping you here on my mother, while she went gallivanting into darkest Africa with Uncle Andrew, on the grounds it was your home. And Vera would never duck a challenge like that.

Vivien does not speak. Allan continues silkily.

ALLAN: What I need to know is - does this unfortunate arrangement continue into the next generation? And if so, what do we do about it?

VIVIEN: I have no idea.

ALLAN: Grace is - nearly eighty and... fragile. She has had one stroke... Vera will obviously go on for ever.

VIVIEN: *(With contempt)* Is that why you're here? Mother said you were after something. What are you trying to do? Get Grace to leave you her share, or change her will if she's left it to me?

ALLAN: That would be ideal. But it's probably too much to hope for. No. I was merely going to ask you to sell me your share of the house. At a family price of course. I haven't any money.

VIVIEN: It's not mine to sell.

ALLAN: Yet.

VIVIEN: She might leave it to the Missionary Society.

ALLAN: To get at Vera? Mmm. That would be a shame. Think about it, anyway, Vivien. I am living here at the moment. Sponging on my Mother because I am flat broke. Annette is no longer satisfied with a separation. She wants a divorce. She'll be a damn sight more expensive than she ever was as a wife. Vera is torn between her Christian abhorrence of divorce and her delight that I have escaped from 'that woman.'

VIVIEN: I'm not asking Grace about her will. Not now.

ALLAN: Isn't that rather sentimental of you?

VIVIEN: She may have left it to Vera anyway.

ALLAN: Do you think so? That would be the best possible solution. Then I'd get the lot for nothing. But Vera would probably drive her into changing her will before -

He stops.

VIVIEN: - before she'd managed to convince everyone that Grace was senile. You are disgusting.

ALLAN: A moral stance is always easy for the uninvolved. Are you going to take over looking after Grace?

Vivien does not answer. Allan smiles.

ALLAN: Exactly. Oh well, I shall have to put mother onto it. Rather a blunt instrument but my case is desperate. But she has always been most careful to demonstrate that my needs come before anyone else's - especially yours.

VIVIEN: *(Drily)* Yes. I remember. Grace could live for another ten years.

ALLAN: Then I am in trouble.

VIVIEN: I'm not going to enter into any sordid negotiations while my mother is - I thought that vultures generally waited till their prey was dead.

ALLAN: Thank you for your co-operation. By all means insult me if it makes you feel better. As it happens I am extremely fond of Grace. I don't think she would be so squeamish - in your shoes. What will you do if Vera, who is no longer young - as she never tires of telling us - finds she cannot cope any more and has to find a good Christian Sunset Home for Grace?

VIVIEN: Allan. You wouldn't!

ALLAN: I shouldn't think it will be necessary. Their mutual loathing should do it for me. Such a bind to have to pretend to get on with your relatives isn't it? 'So is the will of a living daughter curbed by the Will of a dead father.' Or in our case, mother. Dead. Or dying.

VIVIEN: I wish you'd go away, you contemptible little creep.

ALLAN: *(Softly)* Missionary's little girl. Why is everybody so hypocritical about the elderly and their property? I think I'll stroll down and see if they're coming back yet. I'll give Mother a hand with Grace's wheelchair up the hill.

He goes out. Vivien crosses to the bed-settee and yanks it open. It sticks and she has to tug at it. It opens half way. She attacks it fiercely and childishly, kicking and dragging at it until she has it open.

VIVIEN: Stupid bloody thing! Will you - open !!

At last she has the settee open. She picks up the cushions from the sofa and pulls off the cushion covers revealing the pillows beneath. She throws the pillows onto the bed, takes off her coat and hangs it up, draws the curtains to, across the window, then kicks off her shoes and stretches out on the bed. She switches on the bedside light and takes a book from her bag but does not open it. She remains half sitting looking round the room.

VIVIEN: Vivien Chadwick. Just passing through.

After a moment she switches off the bedside light. The lights fade on the rest of the set. After a moment the door opens. There is a shaft of light through the open door and Grace is seen silhouetted against the light. She is leaning heavily on two sticks. She takes a few careful steps into the room. She does not switch on the light, but moves to the window and pulls back the curtains. It is almost dawn and a pearly grey light seeps into the room, obscuring all the detail and making a ghostly presence of Grace in her night-gown. She moves carefully and painfully towards the bed. She stops still, wearied by the effort of walking and seems almost surprised that the sofa is being used as a bed.

GRACE: Vivien! Are you asleep?

There is no answer.

Or are you pretending? That was one of your more maddening habits when you were a girl... Lying with the pillow half over your head. Not a very dignified way for a middle-aged woman to sleep is it? You're lucky to be able to sleep at all... To lead the kind of life that makes you healthily tired... Don't you wake in the small hours? Suddenly wake up. Suddenly snapped wide-awake with no hope of sleeping again? That's when you think of dying. When the sun's coming up... Not while it's still dark... That's the really hopeless time.

She brings the two sticks close together and clasps her

hands over them and bends her head as if praying. She speaks with painful intensity, relating the words of the psalm to her own fears and anguish.

GRACE: 'Be not far from me: for trouble is near: for there is none to help... I am poured out like water and all my bones are out of joint: my heart is like wax, it is melted in the midst of my bowels; and thou hast brought me into the dust of death. For dogs have compassed me; the assembly of the wicked have inclosed me... I may tell all my bones; they look and stare upon me... *(With a kind of terror)* Deliver my soul from the sword; my darling from the power of the dog.'

> *A shadow falls across the door and before Grace can turn to see who it is, Vera, also in night-dress and dressing-gown, has snapped on the main overhead light. Harsh and brutal, it dispels the shadows. Vivien sits up in bed, shading her eyes. Grace half sits, half falls onto the end of the bed where she sits, almost cowering, clutching her sticks.*

VERA: I thought so! It's finally come to this has it? What do you think you're doing?

GRACE: I - couldn't - sleep...

VERA: Oh, you do realise it's night-time then?

VIVIEN: Vera! *(To Grace)* Are you all right?

VERA: Of course she's not all right. Wandering about in the middle of the night talking gibberish to herself.

GRACE: I was - reciting a Psalm. It was a favourite of Andrew's... You could say I was - saying my prayers.

VERA: Don't talk such rubbish. Decent normal people don't wander round saying their prayers in the middle of the night. You don't believe any of it anyway.

GRACE: No. I don't believe any of it, but - some things are horribly true. It's the only time... 'Thou shalt not be afraid of the terror by night' -

> *She looks at Vera, then at Vivien and begins to laugh.*

71

'Nor for the pestilence that walketh in darkness'

She is laughing helplessly. After a moment Vivien joins in.

VIVIEN: 'Nor for the Destruction that wasteth at noonday'.

Vivien and Gace are helpless with laughter.

GRACE: Oh Vera, which of us do you think it is?

VERA: That will do. I had enough of this with Mummy. Even at her worst she didn't - blaspheme. I don't see that there's anything for you to laugh at, Vivien. Perhaps you can see now. It's exactly like Mummy. I know the signs. I didn't sleep for three years. She'd be down in the kitchen making scones at three o' clock in the morning or wandering off down the village in her night-dress. And she was - violent. Dear gentle Mummy. She didn't know me. She didn't know anyone. She didn't know what she was doing. Do you think I want to see my sister go the same way?

VIVIEN: Vera. You must stop this. There's no fear of that.

VERA: Of course there is! Look at her! She can't walk in the daytime. That's the cunning of it. She pretends to be helpless. She won't even try for me.

GRACE: Vera. My dear. You mustn't worry. As far as I can tell at the moment I am not getting like Mother. It's my body that won't work not my mind. That's why I get - bad-tempered. I can't sleep because I don't move all day! Tonight I felt I could. I wanted to see if I could walk. I couldn't wait till morning. And I didn't want all of you fussing round me... I'd forgotten Vivien was sleeping in here... Just think for a minute. I've always been very active... Imagine what it's like having to be dependent... I know you don't like me much, Vera, but won't you be happier when you don't have to be my nurse?

VERA: That is a wicked thing to say. You've got a wicked tongue. You're supposed to be my sister. I'm only trying to do what's best for you and you say evil things like that. You don't care who you hurt. And you laugh at the Bible!

Vivien and Grace are careful not to look at one another.

VERA: Oh yes, I know. I'm too stupid to be let in on the joke. I suppose the joke is me.

VIVIEN: No. No it isn't. *(Biting her lip)* I don't know what it is. It's all of us -

She begins to laugh again, then stops herself.

VERA: Well. Do you want me to put you back to bed? I'm not stopping here all night in the cold.

GRACE: No. Thank you very much, Vera. I'll see to myself.

VERA: Hm! Well, Vivien can see to you I suppose. Don't forget to take her to the bathroom first. Goodnight.

She goes out. Pause.

VIVIEN: Do you want to go to bed?

GRACE: Not yet. I probably can see to myself.

Vivien rises and switches off the light. It is getting light fast outside and the room is slowly getting brighter, but it is a cold light.

VIVIEN: How did you manage the stairs?

GRACE: I've - been practising. I just needed to get out of the chair. *(Carefully)* I think I'm probably going to be all right. This time.

VIVIEN: If you are - *(She stops)* When I've got somewhere to live, would you like to come and stay for a while?

Grace smiles ironically.

GRACE: Only if I can manage on my own?

Vivien looks away.

VIVIEN: I can't - be there - to look after you.

Grace smiles.

GRACE: We'll see. I shouldn't think so. We'll probably go on as we are. Then you'll get a 'phone-call from Vera to say 'I think you should come now Vivien. It won't be long.' or 'Vivien, I'm sorry I'm afraid Grace has passed away. It was very peaceful. It's a blessed release.'

VIVIEN: And I shall hear your mocking laughter in the air.

73

GRACE: *(Drily)* If that is what you want to hear, I expect you will.

She begins to struggle to her feet.

VIVIEN: Don't go. Unless you want to. For a moment.

Grace sits still.

GRACE: To exorcise the dawn demons?

VIVIEN: Who for? You or me?

Vivien suddenly stretches out her hand. Grace looks at her quizzically then takes her hand.

GRACE: *(Bleakly)* It's only a gesture.

VIVIEN: I know.

They sit in silence for a moment. It is becoming lighter. The sun is coming up and the light in the room is warmer.

GRACE: 'And they passed over Jordan; by the morning light there lacked not one of them that was not yet over Jordan.'

Slow Fade.

THE END

By the same author

Stage plays

Harvest	Birmingham Repertory Studio Theatre 1980 Ambassadors Theatre, London 1981 Samuel French Ltd. 1982, First Writes 1996
A Lovely Day Tomorrow	Birmingham Repertory Studio Theatre 1983, First Writes 1996
Anna's Room	Birmingham Repertory Studio Theatre 1984 Samuel French Ltd. 1985, First Writes 1996
Weekend Break	Birmingham Repertory Studio Theatre 1985, First Writes 1996

Short plays

Natural Causes	Traverse Theatre, Edinburgh 1967
A Good Close Fit	Close Theatre, Glasgow 1969

Musicals
With Don Taylor (Lyrics) and Charles Young (Music)

The Burston Drum	Waterman's Arts Centre 1988 Samuel French Ltd. 1989
Summer in the Park	Waterman's Arts Centre 1991 Samuel French Ltd. 1991

First Writes Plays and Playscripts

Ellen Dryden   The Power of the Dog
Harvest, and Other Plays
Six Primroses Each and Other Plays
For Young Actors

Lucy Maurice   Indian Summer

Nicholas McInerny   Red Princess

James Saunders   Retreat

Jack Shepherd   Chasing the Moment

Don Taylor   Retreat from Moscow
When the Barbarians Came
The Road to the Sea

First Writes Poetry

Gordon Mason   Stone Circle

Don Taylor   Five Political Poems
A Prospect of Jerusalem

FIRST
WRITES

First Writes Books
was originally launched as
First Writes Publications
in Autumn 1994 by
First Writes Theatre Company Ltd.
to publish new plays and poetry.

Ellen Dryden was born in Warwickshire. After reading English at Oxford, she trained as an actress at the Royal Academy of Dramatic Art. Her first play, **Natural Causes**, was written while she was appearing at the Traverse Theatre, Edinburgh. This was followed by two television plays, **Visitors** and **The Person Responsible**, and numerous radio plays.

Her first full-length stage play, **Harvest**, was directed at the Birmingham Repertory Theatre. The play was subsequently produced at the Ambassadors Theatre, London. **Harvest** was nominated as *Best New Play* and she herself was nominated as *Most Promising Newcomer* in the *Plays and Players* and *Drama* Awards for 1980-1981. Birmingham Repertory Theatre commissioned and produced her next three plays **A Lovely day Tomorrow**, **Anna's Room** and **Weekend Break**.

She lived and worked in West London until moving out to Norfolk in the Autumn of 1995. She was a co-founder and, for ten years, a director of Chiswick Youth Theatre, writing several one-act plays for the young actors, as well as two full-scale musicals, **The Burston Drum** and **Summer in the Park**. She also gained experience as a director - all kinds of theatre from devised plays to full-scale productions.

In 1993, together with Don Taylor and Richard Blake, she formed **First Writes Theatre Company** and continues to work with them in theatre, publishing and radio.

She is married to playwright and director, Don Taylor, and they have a daughter and a son.